21 DAY JOURNAL
ON
THE GOSPEL OF JOHN

A Personal Commentary

Leslie A. Cory

WALDENHOUSE PUBLISHERS, INC.
WALDEN, TENNESSEE

21 Day Journal on the Gospel of John: a personal commentary

Published by Waldenhouse Publishers, Inc.
100 Clegg Street, Signal Mountain, Tennessee 37377 USA
423-886-2721 www.waldenhouse.com
Printed in the United States of America
Type and Design by Karen Paul Stone
ISBN: 978-1-947589-72-8
Library of Congress Control Number: 2023932565
    A commentary on the Gospel of John as recorded in the Holy
    Bible. Written by a layperson, a student of the Bible with no
    formal theological training. -- provided by Publisher.
REL006800 RELIGION/Biblical Commentary/New Testament/Jesus, the Gospels & Acts
REL006710 RELIGION/Biblical Studies/New Testament/Jesus, the Gospels & Acts
REL070000 RELIGION/Christianity/General

All italicized Scripture quoted in this commentary is the *Authorized Standard Version* (ASV) of the Gospel of John. The ASV is in the public domain in the United States. The particular copy used in this commentary was acquired from Bible Gateway.

Unitalicized quotes from Scripture within the text of the commentary are from the *New Living Translation, Second Edition, 2007* by Tyndale House, henceforward designated "NLT," and are marked accordingly.

PREFACE

Why publish a personal commentary? I am writing because I want to share my experiences in studying John. I may never get to sit down with you to study John, but through this journal commentary we can, in a way, study together. John is the book through which God has most deeply touched my life, and I want to share some of what I have experienced.

I wrote this commentary as I studied. When I came upon an incident that raised a question in my mind, I asked the question. If, as I stopped to ponder and pray concerning that incident, I had an answer that satisfied me, I added the answer to the commentary. If I did not come upon an answer right then, I left my question unanswered, something I could continue to ponder. Thus, the commentary contains two kinds of questions: answered and unanswered.

Since issues develop in John as the gospel story develops, I sometimes left an issue only partially explored at one point in the commentary and returned to it later when the Gospel addressed it more fully. Other times, when I thought it would enhance the clarity of my thinking, I addressed an issue as soon as it arose. Overall, I wanted the commentary to unfold with the gospel story in the same sequence that John presented it. I wanted to get everything out of each passage that I could, without rushing into an as-of-yet unexplored passage in order to get more. However, sometimes getting everything out of a passage meant addressing its implications.

The Table of Contents consists of the summary sentences of each of the chapters. I wanted to impress upon my own mind the sequence of the Gospel of John, and compiling the summary sentences into a table of contents, which also serves as an outline of the Gospel, seemed the most effective method.

TABLE OF CONTENTS

JOHN

Chapter 1: From Heaven to Earth: The Son of God, Second Person of the Trinity, is introduced out of eternity, recognized and proclaimed by the Baptist, and calls His disciples. (How little they understood!)

> *John 1 (ASV) 1In the beginning was the Word, and the Word was with God, and the Word was God. 2The same was in the beginning with God. 3All things were made through him; and without him was not anything made that hath been made. 4In him was life; and the life was the light of men.*

When John the Apostle announced, identified, and proclaimed the Word, he brought a new understanding of God into the world. He announced the Second Person of the Trinity, who had always been at work in peoples' lives, but had never been identified. Suddenly there is God in a second person. Look at all He has done, what we owe Him. Suddenly we not only know that He exists, but have the opportunity to know Him personally. He has done a new thing. He has become a man, lived among us, died for us so that we can live, and has offered us an abundant life we could not have imagined would be ours.

> *5And the light shineth in the darkness; and the darkness apprehended it not.*

The tragedy and the joy of the cosmos: We are surrounded by darkness. The darkness cannot comprehend the Light. But the Light has prevailed!

> *6There came a man, sent from God, whose name was John. 7The same came for witness, that he might bear witness of the light, that all might believe through him. 8He was not the light, but came that he might bear witness of the light. 9There was the true light, even the light which lighteth every man, coming into the world. 10He was in the world, and the world was made through him, and the world knew him not. 11He came unto his own, and they that were his own received him not. 12But as many as received him, to them gave he the right to become children of God, even to them that believe on his name: 13who were born, not of blood, nor of the will of the flesh, nor of the will of man, but of God. 14And the Word became flesh, and dwelt among us (and we beheld his glory, glory as of the only begotten from the Father), full of grace and truth. 15John beareth witness of him, and crieth, saying, This was he of whom I said, He that cometh after me is become before me: for he was before me.*

At this point, the Spirit of God was guiding the Baptist and he spoke with certainty. Later, when his ministry had come to an end and the Spirit was no longer upon Him, he had doubts. John was an Old Testament saint. He did not have the indwelling Spirit. But even Christians can allow themselves to be overwhelmed by doubt and despondency.

John the Baptist testified who Jesus was, "[H]e existed long before me." (NLT.) But John was an instrument of

God. He did not fully understand the meaning of his own words. Later, he demanded an explanation because Jesus was not acting in accord with John's personal expectations. And John died before he saw Jesus fulfill both the scriptures and John's own prophecy by dying, rising, and giving us the Holy Spirit.

> *16For of his fulness we all received, and grace for grace. 17For the law was given through Moses; grace and truth came through Jesus Christ. 18No man hath seen God at any time; the only begotten Son, who is in the bosom of the Father, he hath declared him.*

We cannot see God the Father. We can see Jesus, God the Son. Oh, how He has blessed us by taking on human form! An incalculable gain to us and what a sacrifice for Him! We are not worthy of Your sacrifice, Lord, but You say we are worth it.

> *19And this is the witness of John, when the Jews sent unto him from Jerusalem priests and Levites to ask him, Who art thou? 20And he confessed, and denied not; and he confessed, I am not the Christ. 21And they asked him, What then? Art thou Elijah? And he saith, I am not. Art thou the prophet? And he answered, No. 22They said therefore unto him, Who art thou? that we may give an answer to them that sent us. What sayest thou of thyself? 23He said, I am the voice of one crying in the wilderness, Make straight the way of the Lord, as said Isaiah the prophet. 24And they had been sent from the Pharisees. 25And they asked him, and said unto him, Why then baptizest thou, if thou art not the Christ, neither Elijah, neither the proph-*

*et? 26John answered them, saying, I baptize in water:
in the midst of you standeth one whom ye know not,
27even he that cometh after me, the latchet of whose
shoe I am not worthy to unloose. 28These things were
done in Bethany beyond the Jordan, where John was
baptizing.*

I think Jesus' temptation in the wilderness must have occurred prior to this confrontation between John the Baptist and those sent from the Pharisees. The Gospel of John
does not record Jesus' baptism, but only John the Baptist's
recollection of it. Jesus would have received John's baptism and then been driven into the wilderness by the Holy
Spirit, where He was tempted. Then fully prepared to take
on His ministry, He returned to the place where John the
Baptist was baptizing, in order to start collecting His disciples.

*29On the morrow he seeth Jesus coming unto him,
and saith, Behold, the Lamb of God, that taketh away
the sin of the world! 30This is he of whom I said, After me cometh a man who is become before me: for
he was before me. 31And I knew him not; but that
he should be made manifest to Israel, for this cause
came I baptizing in water. 32And John bare witness,
saying, I have beheld the Spirit descending as a dove
out of heaven; and it abode upon him. 33And I knew
him not: but he that sent me to baptize in water, he
said unto me, Upon whomsoever thou shalt see the
Spirit descending, and abiding upon him, the same is
he that baptizeth in the Holy Spirit.*

Who saw the Spirit descend on Jesus? The Baptist and Jesus, for certain. Was the Spirit visible to anyone else?

34And I have seen, and have borne witness that this is the Son of God.

John identified "the Lamb of God," not because Jesus stood out in the crowd but because God said, this is He. The Spirit rested on Jesus; and Jesus is the One who will give the Spirit to us.

35Again on the morrow John was standing, and two of his disciples; 36and he looked upon Jesus as he walked, and saith, Behold, the Lamb of God! 37And the two disciples heard him speak,

Was one of these disciples John, our author? John was very modest. He would not mention himself by name, but if it had been someone else, he would have said who it was.

and they followed Jesus. 38And Jesus turned, and beheld them following, and saith unto them, What seek ye?

They are seeking their Savior, but they are too shy and uncertain to give an honest answer.

And they said unto him, Rabbi (which is to say, being interpreted, Teacher), where abideth thou? 39He saith unto them, Come, and ye shall see.

Jesus is very gracious to seekers.

They came therefore and saw where he abode; and they abode with him that day: it was about the tenth hour. 40One of the two that heard John speak, and followed him, was Andrew, Simon Peter's brother. 41He findeth first his own brother Simon, and saith unto him, We have found the Messiah (which is, being interpreted, Christ). 42He brought him unto Jesus.

Jesus looked upon him, and said, Thou art Simon the son of John: thou shalt be called Cephas (which is by interpretation, Peter).

To the end of their days on earth these disciples would remember this time and bask in the joy of its promise.

43On the morrow he was minded to go forth into Galilee, and he findeth Philip: and Jesus saith unto him, Follow me.

Jesus is already following the agenda His Father mapped out for Him. He will not leave Bethany beyond the Jordan without Phillip (and Nathanael).

44Now Philip was from Bethsaida, of the city of Andrew and Peter. 45Philip findeth Nathanael, and saith unto him, We have found him, of whom Moses in the law, and the prophets, wrote, Jesus of Nazareth, the son of Joseph. 46And Nathanael said unto him, Can any good thing come out of Nazareth?

"Jesus of Nazareth, the son of Joseph." That is what Philip thought he knew about the facts of Jesus' personal history. By themselves, these facts didn't provide much support for Philip's claim that he had found the Messiah.

Philip saith unto him, Come and see. 47Jesus saw Nathanael coming to him, and saith of him, Behold, an Israelite indeed, in whom is no guile! 48Nathanael saith unto him, Whence knowest thou me? Jesus answered and said unto him, Before Philip called thee, when thou wast under the fig tree, I saw thee. 49Nathanael answered him, Rabbi, thou art the Son of God; thou art King of Israel.

Nathaniel identifies Jesus as "the Son of God" and "the King of Israel." Although Peter gets the credit later on for being the first to comprehend who Jesus really is, John the Baptist had already implanted the expectation in his disciples' minds. Nathaniel was already awaiting the Son of God – the one who existed before John and who would baptize with the Holy Spirit. He followed Jesus in that expectation.

> *50Jesus answered and said unto him, Because I said unto thee, I saw thee underneath the fig tree, believest thou?*

Jesus' statement was a small miracle, but it was one designed specifically for Nathanael. Jesus is saving the world one soul at a time.

> *thou shalt see greater things than these. 51And he saith unto him, Verily, verily, I say unto you, Ye shall see the heaven opened, and the angels of God ascending and descending upon the Son of man.*

Jesus identifies Himself as the stairway between heaven and earth, but in the vision Jacob identified only the angels on the stairway. What did Jacob think of the stairway itself?

Who was with Jesus when He left Bethany for Galilee? Simon and Andrew, Philip and Nathaniel, probably James and John. Anyone else?

Chapter 2: From the security of family to the insecurity of the world: Jesus' mom and the Jewish religious leaders. "I am God and there is no other." Jesus claims authority to change God's mind and to rule over Israel's religious life.

John 2 (ASV) 1And the third day

The third day from what? The third day after Nathaniel's declaration?

> *there was a marriage in Cana of Galilee; and the mother of Jesus was there: 2and Jesus also was bidden, and his disciples, to the marriage. 3And when the wine failed, the mother of Jesus saith unto him, They have no wine. 4And Jesus saith unto her, Woman, what have I to do with thee? mine hour is not yet come. 5His mother saith unto the servants, Whatsoever he saith unto you, do it. 6Now there were six waterpots of stone set there after the Jews' manner of purifying, containing two or three firkins apiece. 7Jesus saith unto them, Fill the waterpots with water. And they filled them up to the brim. 8And he saith unto them, Draw out now, and bear unto the ruler of the feast. And they bare it. 9And when the ruler of the feast tasted the water now become wine, and knew not whence it was (but the servants that had drawn the water knew), the ruler of the feast calleth the bride-*

groom,   10and saith unto him, Every man setteth on first the good wine; and when men have drunk freely, then that which is worse: thou hast kept the good wine until now. 11This beginning of his signs did Jesus in Cana of Galilee, and manifested his glory; and his disciples believed on him.

12After this he went down to Capernaum, he, and his mother, and his brethren, and his disciples; and there they abode not many days.

The miracle at Cana: (a) why was it not Jesus' "time" and (b) why did He do the miracle anyway? Did His "time" begin when He announced His ministry publicly at Jerusalem? (a) Between His baptism and Jerusalem Jesus was transitioning from His role of being the perfect ordinary Jewish guy, obedient to family and cultural norms, to His role of being the iconoclastic God become flesh for all the world to see and believe – or not. For Him, that transition did not include a miracle in Cana of Galilee. His ministry had not begun. (b) But God is always willing to change His mind, to help and encourage those who rely on Him wholly. God has no difficulty reconciling Providence with answered prayer. Did God know Mary would make this request? Of course. God has written the prayers of His people into His story. This apparently unscripted miracle became one of Jesus' pivotal "signs," led His disciples to faith, and has inspired generations of believers.

13And the passover of the Jews was at hand, and Jesus went up to Jerusalem. 14And he found in the temple those that sold oxen and sheep and doves, and the changers of money sitting: 15and he made a scourge of cords, and cast all out of the temple, both the sheep and the oxen; and he poured out the changers' money, and overthrew their tables; 16and to them that sold the doves he said, Take these things hence; make not my Father's house a house of merchandise. 17His disciples remembered that it was written, Zeal for thy house shall eat me up.

Cleansing the Temple. What a perfect way to announce Himself! Actions convey a stronger message than words, when they are the right actions. What stronger statement could an ordinary Jewish man make to pass judgment on Israel's violation of its covenant with God? Everyone, even the priests, knew He was right. They had defiled the Temple and their relationship with God, inviting in the world, the flesh, and the devil. Everyone knew, but only Jesus claimed the authority to do something about it. (I've always liked that Jesus didn't drive out the doves, or overturn the dove sellers' tables. He just told them to leave. He who has His eye on the sparrow watches out for doves, too.)

18The Jews therefore answered and said unto him, What sign showest thou unto us, seeing that thou doest these things?

They asked this when He had not yet performed any signs in Jerusalem. Later, after He showed them untold numbers of signs and miracles, they still asked the same question.

19Jesus answered and said unto them, Destroy this temple, and in three days I will raise it up. 20The Jews therefore said, Forty and six years was this temple in building, and wilt thou raise it up in three days? 21But he spake of the temple of his body. 22When therefore he was raised from the dead, his disciples remembered that he spake this; and they believed the scripture, and the word which Jesus had said.

He predicts His murder at the very beginning of His public ministry. The question some people ask, "Did Jesus have to die?" is absurd to the point of blasphemy. His death was foreordained before the world was created. It was never a matter of human decision. Did humans commit the murder? Yes. Are they responsible for the murder? Yes. We are accountable, but God is in control.

23Now when he was in Jerusalem at the passover, during the feast, many believed on his name, beholding his signs which he did.

Already, at this beginning stage of His ministry, people see His signs and believe on His name. John doesn't tell us what signs Jesus did, but they must have been many and they must have been impressive. To those who were willing to accept the truth, Jesus' miracles proclaimed Him to be what Philip had announced to Nathaniel, "… him, of whom Moses in the law, and the prophets, wrote."

24But Jesus did not trust himself unto them, for that he knew all men, 25and because he needed not that any one should bear witness concerning man; for he himself knew what was in man.

Again, Jesus knew the end from the beginning: man is depraved and only God can rescue him. Jesus is not surprised when I am bad. He already knows what is in me.

Chapter 3: Jesus in the Old Testament through the eyes of doubt and through the eyes of faith: Nicodemus and the Baptist. The line is drawn.

> *John 3 (ASV) 1Now there was a man of the Pharisees, named Nicodemus, a ruler of the Jews: 2the same came unto him by night, and said to him, Rabbi, we know that thou art a teacher come from God; for no one can do these signs that thou doest, except God be with him. 3Jesus answered and said unto him, Verily, verily, I say unto thee, Except one be born anew, he cannot see the kingdom of God.*

What is Nicodemus seeking? He doesn't say. But Jesus knows.

> *4Nicodemus saith unto him, How can a man be born when he is old? can he enter a second time into his mother's womb, and be born?*

This is a stalling tactic. Nicodemus feels he should be in control of the conversation, but he is out of his depth after Jesus' opening remark.

> *5Jesus answered, Verily, verily, I say unto thee, Except one be born of water and the Spirit, he cannot enter into the kingdom of God! 6That which is born of the flesh is flesh; and that which is born of the Spirit is spirit. 7Marvel not that I said unto thee, Ye must be born anew. 8The wind bloweth where it will, and thou*

hearest the voice thereof, but knowest not whence it cometh, and whither it goeth: so is every one that is born of the Spirit.

Even we who are saved, who have been born again, cannot understand the mechanics of how it happens. We only know that it is the work of the Holy Spirit.

9Nicodemus answered and said unto him, How can these things be? 10Jesus answered and said unto him, Art thou the teacher of Israel, and understandest not these things? 11Verily, verily, I say unto thee, We speak that which we know, and bear witness of that which we have seen; and ye receive not our witness. 12If I told you earthly things and ye believe not, how shall ye believe if I tell you heavenly things? 13And no one hath ascended into heaven, but he that descended out of heaven, even the Son of man, who is in heaven. 14And as Moses lifted up the serpent in the wilderness, even so must the Son of man be lifted up; 15that whosoever believeth may in him have eternal life.

Jesus told Nicodemus that to be saved he had to be born again. And he pointed to the future day of his crucifixion, when He would be lifted up for the salvation of the world. Could Nicodemus be "born again" before Jesus' death and resurrection? If not, why did Jesus expect Nicodemus to know this truth already? The truth that should have been clear to Nicodemus from scripture was that he would not – could not – be saved by his own works of righteousness, but only by faith in God and God's willingness to save those who look to Him. Jesus didn't expect Nicodemus to understand how it happened; only that it did.

When Jesus said, "And no one hath ascended into heaven, but he that descended out of heaven, even the Son of man, who is in heaven," what did He mean? How was He in Heaven, while He was on Earth? Was He in Heaven as the eternal Son of God and on Earth as the Son of Man? Or was Heaven so near that He was in Heaven and those around Him could not perceive it? Or was He referencing His future ascension as though it had already occurred? In the economy of God, it had already occurred, hadn't it? The past, present, and future are all before Him.

> 16For God so loved the world, that he gave his only begotten Son, that whosoever believeth on him should not perish, but have eternal life. 17For God sent not the Son into the world to judge the world; but that the world should be saved through him. 18He that believeth on him is not judged: he that believeth not hath been judged already, because he hath not believed on the name of the only begotten Son of God. 19And this is the judgment, that the light is come into the world, and men loved the darkness rather than the light; for their works were evil.

The "judgment" is the separation of those who believe and are saved from those who are not.

> 20For every one that doeth evil hateth the light, and cometh not to the light, lest his works should be reproved. 21But he that doeth the truth cometh to the light, that his works may be made manifest, that they have been wrought in God.

Jesus was a mystery to Nicodemus, but Jesus understood Nicodemus perfectly. Jesus' statement, "You must be born again," was clearly metaphorical, so why did Nicodemus misunderstand it? Out of extreme defensiveness – he could not rebut Jesus' argument, so he tried to deflect it. Nicodemus' following the law would not save him – everything he understood and practiced and revered his whole life was insufficient. Only accepting Jesus' gift of new spiritual life through the work of the Spirit could do it. Man and his ways had been condemned; only by accepting Jesus as Savior could Nicodemus be saved. The validity of the way Jesus offered was established in history – the only way the Israelites were saved from the sting of the serpents was by looking in faith to the serpent on the pole lifted up by Moses. Just so, Nicodemus and all people could be saved by looking to Jesus on the cross for them and trusting in Him. Jesus the Man was the bridge, the stairway, abiding both in Heaven with the Father and on Earth, offering the way into the Father's presence. Those who hate the light of God turn away from Jesus. Those who seek the light of God, turn to Jesus.

Those who go to hell are twice condemned. They are condemned as sinners. They are condemned because they rejected the offer of salvation. The judgment is not final until this second rejection.

> 22After these things came Jesus and his disciples into the land of Judea; and there he tarried with them, and baptized. 23And John also was baptizing in Enon near to Salim, because there was much water there: and they came, and were baptized. 24For John was not yet cast into prison. 25There arose therefore a questioning on the part of John's disciples with a

Jew about purifying. 26And they came unto John, and said to him, Rabbi, he that was with thee beyond the Jordan, to whom thou hast borne witness, behold, the same baptizeth, and all men come to him. 27John answered and said, A man can receive nothing, except it have been given him from heaven. 28Ye yourselves bear me witness, that I said, I am not the Christ, but, that I am sent before him. 29He that hath the bride is the bridegroom: but the friend of the bridegroom, that standeth and heareth him, rejoiceth greatly because of the bridegroom's voice: this my joy therefore is made full. 30He must increase, but I must decrease.

31He that cometh from above is above all: he that is of the earth is of the earth, and of the earth he speaketh: he that cometh from heaven is above all. 32What he hath seen and heard, of that he beareth witness; and no man receiveth his witness.

Receiving His witness is a gift of God. Man cannot acquire it on his own.

33He that hath received his witness hath set his seal to this, that God is true. 34For he whom God hath sent speaketh the words of God: for he giveth not the Spirit by measure. 35The Father loveth the Son, and hath given all things into his hand. 36He that believeth on the Son hath eternal life; but he that obeyeth not the Son shall not see life, but the wrath of God abideth on him.

John the Baptist understood. He was the culmination of human effort reaching out toward God, and he knew he needed a Savior from heaven to provide his salvation. John could show people the need for repentance, but only Christ could save them. Only Christ had the words of eternal life. John saw what Nicodemus did not.

Chapter 4 : Israel redeemed: The Samaritan woman and the Galilean official.

[Review of John's recounting of Jesus' path from baptism to His appointments at Sychar and Cana: Bethany beyond Jordan, Cana, Capernaum, Jerusalem, Judean countryside, Sychar, Cana.]

> *John 4 (ASV) 1When therefore the Lord knew that the Pharisees had heard that Jesus was making and baptizing more disciples than John 2(although Jesus himself baptized not, but his disciples), 3he left Judea, and departed again into Galilee.*

John calls Jesus "Lord." When did he make this discovery? Was it before or after the Resurrection? Only the Spirit could have taught him.

> *4And he must needs pass through Samaria. 5so he cometh to a city of Samaria, called Sychar, near to the parcel of ground that Jacob gave to his son Joseph: 6and Jacob's well was there. Jesus therefore, being wearied with his journey, sat thus by the well. It was about the sixth hour.*

Jesus is tired, but probably no more tired than His disciples. Unlike them, Jesus has a reason to stay at the well. The disciples want to go into town for food and take Jesus' motive for staying to be His fatigue, but Jesus has an appointment. In fact, this meeting had been scheduled since the beginning of time.

7There cometh a woman of Samaria to draw water: Jesus saith unto her, Give me to drink. 8For his disciples were gone away into the city to buy food. 9The Samaritan woman therefore saith unto him, How is it that thou, being a Jew, askest drink of me, who am a Samaritan woman? (For Jews have no dealings with Samaritans.) 10Jesus answered and said unto her, If thou knewest the gift of God, and who it is that saith to thee, Give me to drink; thou wouldest have asked of him, and he would have given thee living water. 11The woman saith unto him, Sir, thou hast nothing to draw with, and the well is deep: whence then hast thou that living water? 12Art thou greater than our father Jacob, who gave us the well, and drank thereof himself, and his sons, and his cattle?

The woman has every reason to understand Jesus literally at first – the subject really was water. Compared to Nicodemus, she catches on fast. Her claim to being a descendent of Jacob is important to her and she asserts it to Jesus.

13Jesus answered and said unto her, Every one that drinketh of this water shall thirst again: 14but whosoever drinketh of the water that I shall give him shall never thirst; but the water that I shall give him shall become in him a well of water springing up unto eternal life. 15The woman saith unto him, Sir, give me this water, that I thirst not, neither come all the way hither to draw.

Yes, Lord, give me this water! She is still keeping her end of the conversation literal, leaving the heavy lifting to Jesus. Perhaps she is defensive. I would have been.

16Jesus saith unto her, Go, call thy husband, and come hither. 17The woman answered and said unto him, I have no husband. Jesus saith unto her, Thou saidst well, I have no husband: 18for thou hast had five husbands; and he whom thou now hast is not thy husband: this hast thou said truly.

If she was already defensive about her spiritual heritage, Jesus' turning to her personal life would have breached her defenses completely. Jesus nailed her – not only with her sin but also with the conviction of His spiritual authority and the importance of this moment.

19The woman saith unto him, Sir, I perceive that thou art a prophet.

The woman is not evading the subject, although she is turning it back to less uncomfortable ground. When she perceives Jesus to be a prophet she asks Him about what is to her the most burning religious issue – whose religion is the right one, the Jews' or the Samaritans'? The perfect point at which to explain true "religion." She is ready to hear.

20Our fathers worshipped in this mountain; and ye say, that in Jerusalem is the place where men ought to worship. 21Jesus saith unto her, Woman, believe me, the hour cometh, when neither in this mountain, nor in Jerusalem, shall ye worship the Father. 22Ye worship that which ye know not: we worship that which we know; for salvation is from the Jews.

Jesus acknowledges that she worships God (and not a demon), but her religion is deficient in understanding. Jesus took the Samaritans' faith seriously. They believed they were true descendants of Jacob (Israel). They had the Law of Moses. They were the mongrelized descendants of the ten tribes. But they worshiped Whom they did not know.

> *23But the hour cometh, and now is, when the true worshippers shall worship the Father in spirit and truth: for such doth the Father seek to be his worshippers. 24God is a Spirit: and they that worship him must worship in spirit and truth.*

Jesus offers her the opportunity to be the first among her people to worship God in spirit and in truth, wholly and intelligently. She was waiting for Messiah. She was ready for Him. She has found Him.

> *25The woman saith unto him, I know that Messiah cometh (he that is called Christ): when he is come, he will declare unto us all things. 26Jesus saith unto her, I that speak unto thee am he.*

Jesus is calling back the remains of the ten "lost" tribes. This woman is what is left of Israel, after the sins of the nation led to destruction and displacement. (It would be interesting to trace her ancestry back to 722 B.C.) Was Jesus calling the remnants of the Northern Kingdom back, fulfilling the Father's promise that "all Israel be saved"?

> *27And upon this came his disciples; and they marvelled that he was speaking with a woman; yet no man said, What seekest thou? or, Why speakest thou with her? 28So the woman left her waterpot, and went away into the city, and saith to the people, 29Come, see a man, who told me all things that ever I did: can this be the Christ? 30They went out of the city, and*

were coming to him. 31In the mean while the disciples prayed him, saying, Rabbi, eat. 32But he said unto them, I have meat to eat that ye know not. 33The disciples therefore said one to another, Hath any man brought him aught to eat? 34Jesus saith unto them, My meat is to do the will of him that sent me, and to accomplish his work. 35say not ye, There are yet four months, and then cometh the harvest? behold, I say unto you, Lift up your eyes, and look on the fields, that they are white already unto harvest. 36He that reapeth receiveth wages, and gathereth fruit unto life eternal; that he that soweth and he that reapeth may rejoice together. 37For herein is the saying true, One soweth, and another reapeth. 38I sent you to reap that whereon ye have not labored: others have labored, and ye are entered into their labor.

Others had already sowed in Sychar. Jesus' disciples were there to harvest. Who is it who had sowed? Somebody had. In a way Jesus sowed, and in a way the woman sowed. In a way the Old Testament prophets God had sent to the Northern Kingdom sowed. And in a way the Samaritans' Pentateuch sowed. Perhaps there were "others" of God's servants whose work was not recorded in the Old Testament. Perhaps they came during the 400 years after Ezra and Nehemiah had rejected the Samaritans as descendants of Israel and inheritors of the Mosaic traditions. The Samaritans considered themselves children of the Promise. They were awaiting the Messiah. Now He had come to gather His harvest among them.

39And from that city many of the Samaritans believed on him because of the word of the woman, who

*testified, He told me all things that ever I did. 40So
when the Samaritans came unto him, they besought
him to abide with them: and he abode there two days.*

They wanted Him! These people of Samaria welcomed the
Messiah!

*41And many more believed because of his word;
42and they said to the woman, Now we believe, not
because of thy speaking: for we have heard for ourselves, and know that this is indeed the Saviour of the
world.*

Sychar was a village. They begged Him to stay and He did.
Some day I will meet the people of Sychar and the woman
at the well.

*43And after the two days he went forth from thence
into Galilee. 44For Jesus himself testified, that a
prophet hath no honor in his own country.*

Now He will go to His own people and they will reject
Him.

*45So when he came into Galilee, the Galilaeans re-
ceived him, having seen all the things that he did in
Jerusalem at the feast: for they also went unto the
feast.*

The Galileans were excited about Jesus, not because of
the miracles He had performed in Galilee, but because of
what He had done in Jerusalem. Why does a successful
hometown boy provoke such jealousy? Low self-esteem?
Hatred of one's own inadequacies?

*46He came therefore again unto Cana of Galilee,
where he made the water wine. And there was a cer-*

tain nobleman, whose son was sick at Capernaum. 47When he heard that Jesus was come out of Judaea into Galilee, he went unto him, and besought him that he would come down, and heal his son; for he was at the point of death. 48Jesus therefore said unto him, Except ye see signs and wonders, ye will in no wise believe.

Healing the official's son. Galilee accepted Jesus at this point because many had seen His miracles in Jerusalem. The official came in person from Capernaum to Cana to beg Jesus to heal his son. Was Jesus' tart response directed solely to the official, or also to those standing around watching to see what Jesus would do – those who only believed because of the miracles they had witnessed? Jesus spoke the words to the man, so the man must have had the very feelings Jesus described. He came to Jesus not because he had faith, but because Jesus had made a name for Himself in Judea.

49The nobleman saith unto him, Sir, come down ere my child die.

Jesus provoked the man to desperation, into acknowledging his need of The Savior.

50Jesus saith unto him, Go thy way; thy son liveth. The man believed the word that Jesus spake unto him, and he went his way.

51And as he was now going down, his servants met him, saying, that his son lived. 52So he inquired of them the hour when he began to amend. They said therefore unto him, Yesterday at the seventh hour the fever left him. 53So the father knew that it was at that hour in which Jesus said unto him, Thy son liveth: and himself believed, and his whole house.

I have often wondered how long the trip home took and what time the servants met the official. Since a new day started in Galilee at 6PM, what the servants called "yesterday" could have been what to us would be the afternoon of the same day. Perhaps the official started home immediately after speaking with Jesus, his servants started from home as soon as his son was healed, and they met a few hours later, the same day for us, but the next day by Jewish definitions.

54This is again the second sign that Jesus did, having come out of Judaea into Galilee.

John calls this the "second sign" after coming from Judea to Galilee. The first was in Cana after His return from being baptized. The second was in Cana after His return from the Temple. Jesus did other miracles, both in Judea and in Galilee. These two were special signs because they were turning points in His earthly ministry. After each, He went to Jerusalem and asserted His claim as Lord.

Chapter 5: Which side of death are you on? The lame man, the Pharisees, and what is required to pass from condemnation to life.

John 5 (ASV) 1After these things there was a feast of the Jews; and Jesus went up to Jerusalem.

Back to Jerusalem.

2Now there is in Jerusalem by the sheep gate a pool, which is called in Hebrew Bethesda, having five porches. 3In these lay a multitude of them that were sick, blind, halt, withered, waiting for the moving of the water, 4for an angel of the Lord went down at certain seasons into the pool, and troubled the water: whosoever then first after the troubling of the waters stepped in was made whole, with whatsoever disease he was holden. 5And a certain man was there, who had been thirty and eight years in his infirmity. 6 When Jesus saw him lying, and knew that he had been now a long time in that case, he saith unto him, Wouldest thou be made whole? 7The sick man answered him, Sir, I have no man, when the water is troubled, to put me into the pool: but while I am coming, another steppeth down before me. 8Jesus saith unto him, Arise, take up thy bed, and walk. 9And straightway the man was made whole, and took up his bed and walked.

This man did not even know Jesus. He did not ask for help. Jesus came to Him and offered help. Although the man never asked for Jesus' help, he accepted the good thing that Jesus did for him. Do I do this? Fail to seek Jesus' help when I need it and then fail to acknowledge His mercy after I receive it?

> *Now it was the sabbath on that day. 10So the Jews said unto him that was cured, It is the sabbath, and it is not lawful for thee to take up thy bed. 11But he answered them, He that made me whole, the same said unto me, Take up thy bed, and walk. 12They asked him, Who is the man that said unto thee, Take up thy bed, and walk? 13But he that was healed knew not who it was; for Jesus had conveyed himself away, a multitude being in the place. 14Afterward Jesus findeth him in the temple, and said unto him, Behold, thou art made whole: sin no more, lest a worse thing befall thee. 15The man went away, and told the Jews that it was Jesus who had made him whole.*

Why did Jesus heal this man? Was it out of compassion? Jesus certainly meant to provoke the Pharisees, but what was His intention toward the man? The man did follow Jesus' instructions. He picked up his mat and walked. But when challenged by the Pharisees about working on the Sabbath, he made a point of giving Jesus up. He put his Healer in harm's way in order to preserve his own security. And this was after Jesus had given him a stern warning, "Now you are well; so stop sinning, or something even worse may happen to you." If the lame man had believed Jesus at the start, Jesus would not have needed to warn him of the fate that awaited him – the man would already have passed from death to life. The man feared the Pharisees more than he feared Jesus or the power of God, so gave Jesus up to them. He had a choice. Even had he not repented, he could have gone on with his life, hidden from the Pharisees after they released him, but instead he went back to them, to point the finger at Jesus. Was it fear that sent him back to curry favor with the Pharisees? Might I have done the same thing? Save yourself by laying the blame on someone else. I have done it. What cowards we can be!

> *16And for this cause the Jews persecuted Jesus because he did these things on the sabbath. 17But Jesus answered them, My Father worketh even until now, and I work. 18For this cause therefore the Jews sought the more to kill him, because he not only brake the sabbath, but also called God his own Father, making himself equal with God.*

Jesus' answer to the Pharisees: "My Father is always working, and so am I." (NLT.) The Sabbath controversy – God is working all the time. Jesus attributed to God a power that apparently the Pharisees did not – the power to maintain the physical universe, all of nature, at all times. God rested from His creation of the cosmos on Saturday, but He has never rested from sustaining it.

> *19Jesus therefore answered and said unto them, Verily, verily, I say unto you, The Son can do nothing of himself, but what he seeth the Father doing: for what things soever he doeth, these the Son also doeth in like manner.*

Are we to imitate the Father also, in the way we handle the "Sabbath"?

20For the Father loveth the Son, and showeth him all things that himself doeth: and greater works than these will he show him, that ye may marvel. 21For as the Father raiseth the dead and giveth them life, even so the Son also giveth life to whom he will.

What does Jesus mean "… the Father gives life to those He raises from the dead?" (NLT.) Is Jesus speaking of the resurrection of the dead as though it had already happened? For God, it has. He sees the end from the beginning, and for us, God's promise is the same as the fulfillment of the promise. It is certain. But the life Jesus gives, it happens now, doesn't it? We get new bodies later. We get new life now.

22For neither doth the Father judge any man, but he hath given all judgment unto the Son; 23that all may honor the Son, even as they honor the Father. He that honoreth not the Son honoreth not the Father that sent him.

"In addition, the Father judges no one. Instead He has given the Son absolute authority to judge." (NLT.) How this must have set off the Pharisees. They expected God to treat them well when they were judged. But they knew how Jesus regarded them. They would not expect to fare well in a court over which Jesus presided.

24Verily, verily, I say unto you, He that heareth my word, and believeth him that sent me, hath eternal life, and cometh not into judgment, but hath passed out of death into life.

What is the basis for Jesus' judgment? "… those who listen to my voice and believe in God who sent me have eternal life. They will never be condemned for their sins, but they have already passed from death to life." (NLT.) They will not be condemned because Jesus will be / already has been condemned in their place. Those who believed Jesus' message when He spoke it then were saved, just as we, on this side of the cross, who believe, are saved.

> 25Verily, verily, I say unto you, The hour cometh, and now is, when the dead shall hear the voice of the Son of God; and they that hear shall live.

"… the time … it's here now …" (NLT), when sinners will hear and believe and pass from death to life. The Son judges and the Son gives life. This is what we are all waiting for, the Words that give us life.

> 26For as the Father hath life in himself, even so gave he to the Son also to have life in himself: 27and he gave him authority to execute judgment, because he is a son of man.

Jesus has the authority because He did the work that accomplished our salvation.

> 28Marvel not at this: for the hour cometh, in which all that are in the tombs shall hear his voice, 29and shall come forth; they that have done good, unto the resurrection of life; and they that have done evil, unto the resurrection of judgment.

> 30I can of myself do nothing: as I hear, I judge: and my judgment is righteous; because I seek not mine own will, but the will of him that sent me.

Jesus predicts it is His voice that will precipitate the general resurrection. "… those who have done good …" vs "those who have continued in evil ...." (NLT.) Everyone has a choice. Those who continue in evil after they have the opportunity to choose Jesus will be condemned. This is the Father's decree and Jesus will carry it out. Those who have "done good" are those who, as Jesus announced in verse 24, are those who listened and believed. They were not saved by their own good works, but when they listened and believed in Jesus and His saving power, a work was done in them and it was very good.

> *31If I bear witness of myself, my witness is not true. 32It is another that beareth witness of me; and I know that the witness which he witnesseth of me is true. 33Ye have sent unto John, and he hath borne witness unto the truth. 34But the witness which I receive is not from man: howbeit I say these things, that ye may be saved. 35He was the lamp that burneth and shineth; and ye were willing to rejoice for a season in his light.*

Jesus references John because the people esteemed John's witness. Jesus' more powerful witnesses, as He now says, are His miracles, which could be wrought only by God, and the Old Testament scriptures, which spoke of Him.

> *36But the witness which I have is greater than that of John; for the works which the Father hath given me to accomplish, the very works that I do, bear witness of me, that the Father hath sent me. 37And the Father that sent me, he hath borne witness of me. Ye have neither heard his voice at any time, nor seen his form.*

They who claimed to be God's people had failed to hear God's voice, but they had seen Jesus' miracles with their own eyes. Even those ignorant of the scriptures could see

His miracles. Jesus offered proof, and anyone with an open mind would have believed His miracles demonstrated He was from God.

> *38And ye have not his word abiding in you: for whom he sent, him ye believe not. 39Ye search the scriptures, because ye think that in them ye have eternal life; and these are they which bear witness of me; 40and ye will not come to me, that ye may have life.*

This is knowing, willful rejection of God.

> *41I receive not glory from men. 42But I know you, that ye have not the love of God in yourselves. 43I am come in my Father's name, and ye receive me not: if another shall come in his own name, him ye will receive. 44How can ye believe, who receive glory one of another, and the glory that cometh from the only God ye seek not?*

This is the way of man, when left to his own devices.

> *45Think not that I will accuse you to the Father: there is one that accuseth you, even Moses, on whom ye have set your hope. 46For if ye believed Moses, ye would believe me; for he wrote of me. 47But if ye believe not his writings, how shall ye believe my words?*

Jesus gave His hearers an opportunity to be saved – that's why He bothered to explain things to them. John the Baptist brought about a little stirring in their souls; Jesus' testimony from the Father was far greater than John's; why wouldn't the Pharisees believe? They believed they owned the Bible and its contents, and they never saw Jesus there. They were unwilling to see Him there, even when He opened the Bible to them. They wanted the honor due to Jesus, and they honored each other in order to receive honor themselves. They rejected the One to whom honor was due – whoever honors Jesus must acknowledge his own unworthiness. This they would not do.

When Jesus accused the Pharisees of not understanding Moses, He attacked them where they were most sensitive – their knowledge of Scripture was their source of pride. What irony – they were condemned before God because of their failure to grasp the truth of the Book they claimed to be their own special domain.

The incident of the healing of the lame man led to uncovering the sin of unbelief among the Pharisees. Chapter 5 tells the stories of the lame man's healing and of Jesus' rebutting the Pharisees' claim to preserving the truth of Scripture. They had preserved the treasure box, but they had not opened it up to benefit from the riches within. On which side of death did the lame man end up – Jesus' or the Pharisees'?

Chapter 6: What are you hungry for? To the far side of the Sea of Galilee and back to Capernaum. Passover on the mountain in Galilee; confrontation in Capernaum. Faith is easy; faith is hard.

> *John 6 (ASV) 1After these things Jesus went away to the other side of the sea of Galilee, which is the sea of Tiberias. 2And a great multitude followed him, because they beheld the signs which he did on them that were sick. 3And Jesus went up into the mountain, and there he sat with his disciples. 4Now the passover, the feast of the Jews, was at hand.*

But Jesus wasn't going to be in Jerusalem for it.

> *5Jesus therefore lifting up his eyes, and seeing that a great multitude cometh unto him, saith unto Philip, Whence are we to buy bread, that these may eat? 6And this he said to prove him: for he himself knew what he would do. 7Philip answered him, Two hundred shillings' worth of bread is not sufficient for them, that every one may take a little.*

Philip answered from the human, carnal, perspective. He still thought as a flesh-bound person, not as a member of the Kingdom. Jesus often tested Philip. But we don't hear about Philip in Acts; we hear about Philip the deacon. What happened to Philip the apostle? Did he travel far? Was he martyred early?

8One of his disciples, Andrew, Simon Peter's brother, saith unto him, 9There is a lad here, who hath five barley loaves, and two fishes: but what are these among so many?

The "lad" was willing to share. Andrew, in a combination of confusion and desire to go where Jesus was leading them, took a stab at answering Jesus' question. The young boy must have heard the discussion about feeding the people and offered his meal to Andrew. How else would Andrew have known the boy had a meal? Andrew felt foolish offering the tiny portion of food, but he also felt compelled to make the boy's offer known to Jesus. Oh, that I would display even that much faith – to step out, even while feeling foolish!

10Jesus said, Make the people sit down. Now there was much grass in the place. So the men sat down, in number about five thousand. 11Jesus therefore took the loaves; and having given thanks, he distributed to them that were set down; likewise also of the fishes as much as they would. 12And when they were filled, he saith unto his disciples, Gather up the broken pieces which remain over, that nothing be lost.

Jesus teaches us to be good stewards of God's blessings. God is extravagant, but not wasteful.

13So they gathered them up, and filled twelve baskets with broken pieces from the five barley loaves, which remained over unto them that had eaten. 14When therefore the people saw the sign which he did, they said, This is of a truth the prophet that cometh into the world.

15Jesus therefore perceiving that they were about to come and take him by force, to make him king, withdrew again into the mountain himself alone.

"When the people saw Him do this miraculous sign, they exclaimed, 'Surely He is the Prophet we have been expecting!' When Jesus saw that there ready to force Him to be king, He slipped away ...." (NLT.) Democracy at work! It didn't matter that Jesus did not want to be their (earthly) king, or that He had other plans. Jesus could produce food and the people somehow thought they could force Him to produce for them. They saw the miracle, but they didn't appreciate the power and purpose behind it. They had come because of the Lord's signs, but once they saw His potential from a material perspective, any spiritual longings were overcome by the logic of the flesh. Our flesh is materialistic. How could it not be? Jesus' flesh submitted to His spirit.

When He fed the people, He knew what their response would be, but He fed them anyway. It all worked into His great plan of salvation.

16And when evening came, his disciples went down unto the sea; 17and they entered into a boat, and were going over the sea unto Capernaum. And it was now dark, and Jesus had not yet come to them. 18And the sea was rising by reason of a great wind that blew. 19When therefore they had rowed about five and twenty or thirty furlongs, they behold Jesus walking on the sea, and drawing nigh unto the boat: and they were afraid. 20But he saith unto them, It is I; be not afraid. 21They were willing therefore to receive him

into the boat: and straightway the boat was at the
land whither they were going.

Why did the disciples leave without Jesus? They waited on
the shore, He didn't come, and they left Him. Had He told
them to leave when it got dark? Had they tarried even after He had told them go? Did they think they weren't safe
on the shore overnight?

There is no description of Peter walking on water in John's
account. John can't be distracted from the message of
Christ our Passover.

> *22On the morrow the multitude that stood on the*
> *other side of the sea saw that there was no other boat*
> *there, save one, and that Jesus entered not with his*
> *disciples into the boat, but that his disciples went*
> *away alone 23(howbeit there came boats from Tibe-*
> *rias nigh unto the place where they ate the bread af-*
> *ter the Lord had given thanks): 24when the multitude*
> *therefore saw that Jesus was not there, neither his dis-*
> *ciples, they themselves got into the boats, and came to*
> *Capernaum, seeking Jesus.*

Surely not all of them got into boats. The crowd arriving
in Capernaum must have been smaller that the crowd that
had been fed.

> *25And when they found him on the other side of the*
> *sea, they said unto him, Rabbi, when camest thou*
> *hither? 26Jesus answered them and said, Verily, ver-*
> *ily, I say unto you, Ye seek me, not because ye saw*
> *signs, but because ye ate of the loaves, and were filled.*
> *27Work not for the food which perisheth, but for the*

food which abideth unto eternal life, which the Son of man shall give unto you: for him the Father, even God, hath sealed.

In verses 26-27 Jesus explains their error and makes an attempt to get through to them. But the crowd wants to be like Jesus in His ability to perform miracles. Because of their greed they have demoted Jesus in their assessment from a miracle worker sent from God to a food service. Jesus' food was to do the will of His Father. After we have fed on Jesus and been brought into new life, that will be our food, as well.

28They said therefore unto him, What must we do, that we may work the works of God? 29Jesus answered and said unto them, This is the work of God, that ye believe on him whom he hath sent. 30They said therefore unto him, What then doest thou for a sign, that we may see, and believe thee? what workest thou?

Did they not just see a sign? Yes, but right now they aren't after proof of who Jesus is. They are trying to manipulate Him into providing their daily bread, just as God did through Moses in the desert.

31Our fathers ate the manna in the wilderness; as it is written, He gave them bread out of heaven to eat. 32Jesus therefore said unto them, Verily, verily, I say unto you, It was not Moses that gave you the bread out of heaven; but my Father giveth you the true bread out of heaven.

Jesus confronts them with what God demands of them (as opposed to their demands of Jesus). They demand food from Jesus in return for their faith! How am I like this? Following Jesus only in expectation of His blessings. Jesus offered them eternal life; they wanted food. Compare their reaction to that of the Samaritan woman at the well. Upon hearing Jesus' offer of living water, she left her water pitcher and ran to her people, so that they could meet their Savior. The Samaritans of Sychar embraced Jesus' offer. Jesus' own people rejected it. Their national pride as the chosen people prevented them from seeing their need.

> *33For the bread of God is that which cometh down out of heaven, and giveth life unto the world. 34They said therefore unto him, Lord, evermore give us this bread. 35Jesus said unto them, I am the bread of life: he that cometh to me shall not hunger, and he that believeth on me shall never thirst.*

This was the same offer Jesus made to the Samaritan woman.

> *36But I said unto you, that ye have seen me, and yet believe not. 37All that which the Father giveth me shall come unto me; and him that cometh to me I will in no wise cast out. 38For I am come down from heaven, not to do mine own will, but the will of him that sent me. 39And this is the will of him that sent me, that of all that which he hath given me I should lose nothing, but should raise it up at the last day. 40For this is the will of my Father, that every one that beholdeth the Son, and believeth on him, should have eternal life; and I will raise him up at the last day.*

Jesus corrected their bad theology, insulted their national pride, and drew the true distinction between the chosen people and the unchosen – belief and unbelief. It was God who fed Israel, not Moses. God will feed them still, true food for their souls, if they would desire God and His food. Jesus explained that His plan and purpose would succeed. Those among the crowd who belong to Jesus would come to Him and He would save them forever.

> *41 The Jews therefore murmured concerning him, because he said, I am the bread which came down out of heaven.*

Those who are not His use their human logic, so limited and faulty, to reject Jesus' claim of having come from God.

> *42And they said, Is not this Jesus, the son of Joseph, whose father and mother we know? how doth he now say, I am come down out of heaven?*

John does not narrate the Virgin Birth in his gospel, but it is clearly a relevant issue.

> *43Jesus answered and said unto them, Murmur not among yourselves. 44No man can come to me, except the Father that sent me draw him: and I will raise him up in the last day. 45It is written in the prophets, And they shall all be taught of God. Every one that hath heard from the Father, and hath learned, cometh unto me. 46Not that any man hath seen the Father, save he that is from God, he hath seen the Father.*

Jesus is the only human being who has ever seen the Father "face to face." (Moses spoke to the Second Person of the Trinity "face to face.")

> *47Verily, verily, I say unto you, He that believeth hath eternal life. 48I am the bread of life. 49Your fathers ate the manna in the wilderness, and they died. 50This is*

the bread which cometh down out of heaven, that a man may eat thereof, and not die. 51I am the living bread which came down out of heaven: if any man eat of this bread, he shall live for ever: yea and the bread which I will give is my flesh, for the life of the world.

52The Jews therefore strove one with another, saying, How can this man give us his flesh to eat?

Jesus was still speaking in metaphors, but the Jews were turning His metaphor into an image that revolted them.

When Jesus describes Himself as the bread of Heaven, people can understand the metaphor. When He says His followers must eat His flesh, the metaphor is more than the crowd can handle. Yet it is the same metaphor, the one they played out every year at Passover. Jesus described His role as the Passover lamb. When the Jews ate the lamb, they knew they were consuming their substitute. By eating the lamb they joined in its death. But here, they are blind to the significance and reality of what they did every year by tradition.

53Jesus therefore said unto them, Verily, verily, I say unto you, Except ye eat the flesh of the Son of man and drink his blood, ye have not life in yourselves. 54He that eateth my flesh and drinketh my blood hath eternal life: and I will raise him up at the last day.

"But anyone who eats My flesh and drinks My blood has eternal life, and I will raise that person on the last day." (NLT.) Surely Jesus knew this would end the conversation. No one would want Him to be king anymore. But He wanted to show them the way to eternal life while He had their attention – it would make sense later, after the resurrection. Why is it that Jesus as the Bread of Heaven that gives eternal life is such a beautiful metaphor, but eating the Bread's flesh is so ugly? Eating is what you do with bread.

> *55For my flesh is meat indeed, and my blood is drink indeed. 56He that eateth my flesh and drinketh my blood abideth in me, and I in him. 57As the living Father sent me, and I live because of the Father; so he that eateth me, he also shall live because of me.*

To come to Jesus we must accept the ugliness of our sin and the horror of Jesus' sacrifice for us – we must accept it, own it, enter into it with Him. Do not rebel when you are confronted with the horror of the death for which you are responsible

> *58This is the bread which came down out of heaven: not as the fathers ate, and died; he that eateth this bread shall live for ever. 59These things said he in the synagogue, as he taught in Capernaum.*
>
> *60Many therefore of his disciples, when the heard this, said, This is a hard saying; who can hear it? 61But Jesus knowing in himself that his disciples murmured at this, said unto them, Doth this cause you to stumble? 62What then if ye should behold the Son of man ascending where he was before? 63It is the spirit that giveth life; the flesh profiteth nothing: the words that I have spoken unto you are spirit, are life. 64But there are some of you that believe not. For Jesus knew from the beginning who they were that believed not, and who it was that should betray him. 65And he said, For this cause have I said unto you, that no man*

*can come unto me, except it be given unto him of the
Father.*

Jesus tells them how they should understand His saying,
but they cannot get past their fleshly understanding of
what He has said. Only those drawn by the Father will per-
severe with Him.

> *66Upon this many of his disciples went back, and
> walked no more with him. 67Jesus said therefore unto
> the twelve, Would ye also go away? 68Simon Peter
> answered him, Lord, to whom shall we go? thou hast
> the words of eternal life. 69And we have believed and
> know that thou art the Holy One of God. 70Jesus an-
> swered them, Did not I choose you the twelve, and one
> of you is a devil? 71Now he spake of Judas the son of
> Simon Iscariot, for he it was that should betray him,
> being one of the twelve.*

Jesus spoke the brutal metaphor for the purpose of sepa-
rating His sheep from the others. He spoke spirit and life,
but only those given Jesus by the Father could accept it.
Try to imagine God's perspective on the life and death of
the human body. Jesus, who created human flesh to start
with and understood the nitrogen cycle very well, had a
different relationship to the word "flesh" than we do. We
nourish our flesh and love it and cannot imagine life without it. To us it may even seem to be the essence of life.
But not so for Jesus. He could offer Himself to us, knowing that our "eating" His "flesh" would in no way diminish
Him. It would make us eternally His. We experience the
horror of Jesus' death for us, but we live in the joy of His
resurrection.

Chapter 7: Can you handle the truth? Jesus and His brothers, Jesus and the people, Jesus and the Jewish leaders: What we think, say, and do are all controlled by our pre-conceptions and personal interests. What power can overcome these influences in our lives?

> *John 7 (ASV) 1And after these things Jesus walked in Galilee: for he would not walk in Judaea, because the Jews sought to kill him. 2Now the feast of the Jews, the feast of tabernacles, was at hand. 3His brethren therefore said unto him, Depart hence, and go into Judaea, that thy disciples also may behold thy works which thou doest. 4For no man doeth anything in secret, and himself seeketh to be known openly. If thou doest these things, manifest thyself to the world. 5For even his brethren did not believe on him.*

This conversation occurred after the "eat my flesh" discourse. Jesus' brothers were fed up with Him and the social stigma they experienced as a result of being related to Him. His brothers had been with Him from the beginning of His ministry. They had seen His miracles, heard His teaching. They knew He had power, but they did not understand Him at all. Was it their familiarity with Him, the kindness and tolerance He had always showed them, that led to their contempt? They hoped to push Him into action, to manipulate Him by attacking His self-esteem. How blind they were, to be taunting God!

> 6Jesus therefore saith unto them, My time is not yet come; but your time is always ready. 7The world cannot hate you; but me it hateth, because I testify of it, that its works are evil. 8Go ye up unto the feast: I go not up unto this feast; because my time is not yet fulfilled. 9And having said these things unto them, he abode still in Galilee.

Why were Jesus' brothers so spiteful and disbelieving? Why did Jesus respond seriously to their taunts?

Jesus' brothers' disbelief was the result of their certainty that if anyone had the power Jesus claimed, He would use it the way they would use it if they had the power. Their mockery was a result of anger that He had let them down and envy of His status in the family. Jesus was a huge family problem. He disrupted all of their lives. They had to change their lifestyle to accommodate His ministry. But He would not take what to them was the next logical step: declare Himself openly as the leader of the people. If He would do that, and succeed, at least His brothers would garner some benefits for all the trouble He caused them. But He remained in a sort of limbo—experiencing all the difficulties and none of the rewards of being a leader. Jesus' brothers had no concept of the Kingdom of Heaven. Like everyone else around Him, their hopes were fixed on a kingdom of this world. Jesus was not meeting their expectations and because He was family, they took advantage of their relationship to mock Him. Rather than fixing their eyes on Jesus and seeking His Kingdom, they chose to remain mired in the world's perspective of reality.

How should you respond when people mock you? You can respond in kind, which may make you look smart, but which brings you down to your attackers' level of pettiness. Or you can ignore the taunts, which may be noble, but leaves the taunters stewing in their resentment. Or you can answer as though your taunters had asked a serious question. Jesus' brothers knew why He didn't go to the feast, but He answered as though they did not. In doing so He exposed their shameful behavior for what it was – a symptom of their enmity with God and their friendship with the world.

> *10But when his brethren were gone up unto the feast, then went he also up, not publicly, but as it were in secret. 11The Jews therefore sought him at the feast, and said, Where is he? 12And there was much murmuring among the multitudes concerning him: some said, He is a good man; others said, Not so, but he leadeth the multitude astray. 13Yet no man spake openly of him for fear of the Jews.*

A divided public. Just like today. Sometimes you have to take a stand. Jesus required it regarding Himself. Inaction on our parts truly can lead to the triumph of chaos and evil. When that happens, we can try to blame others, but the fault is in ourselves.

> *14But when it was now the midst of the feast Jesus went up into the temple, and taught. 15The Jews therefore marvelled, saying, How knoweth this man letters, having never learned? 16Jesus therefore answered them and said, My teaching is not mine, but his that sent me. 17If any man willeth to do his will, he shall know of the teaching, whether it is of God,*

or whether I speak from myself. 18He that speaketh from himself seeketh his own glory: but he that seeketh the glory of him that sent him, the same is true, and no unrighteousness is in him. 19Did not Moses give you the law, and yet none of you doeth the law? Why seek ye to kill me? 20The multitude answered, Thou hast a demon: who seeketh to kill thee? 21Jesus answered and said unto them, I did one work, and ye all marvel because thereof. 22Moses hath given you circumcision (not that it is of Moses, but of the fathers); and on the sabbath ye circumcise a man. 23If a man receiveth circumcision on the sabbath, that the law of Moses may not be broken; are ye wroth with me, because I made a man every whit whole on the sabbath? 24Judge not according to appearance, but judge righteous judgment.

In Jerusalem at the Feast of Booths. Jesus was able to say a lot to the people during this discourse, because they had to figure out who He was from what He was saying. Jesus puts His finger on His brothers' sin, as well as the Jews': "Anyone who wants to do the will of God will know whether my teaching is from God or is merely my own." (NLT.) God will confirm the truth to those who want to know the truth in order to obey the truth. Neither Jesus' brothers nor many in the crowd wanted to obey. They based their conclusions about Jesus on a superficial comparison of Him to their incomplete understanding of scripture and their warped world view.

What was the "one work" Jesus had done? The controversy in Jerusalem is not the same as the one in Galilee. People in Jerusalem don't know all of what has happened in

Galilee. They do know that Jesus healed a crippled man on the Sabbath.

> *25Some therefore of them of Jerusalem said, Is not this he whom they seek to kill? 26And lo, he speaketh openly, and they say nothing unto him. Can it be that the rulers indeed know that this is the Christ? 27Howbeit we know this man whence he is: but when the Christ cometh, no one knoweth whence he is. 28Jesus therefore cried in the temple, teaching and saying, Ye both know me, and know whence I am; and I am not come of myself, but he that sent me is true, whom ye know not. 29I know him; because I am from him, and he sent me.*

John does a great job portraying how crowds process what they are observing. The people meant they knew Jesus was from Galilee. They thought they were not supposed to know where the Messiah was from geographically, and in fact, they did not know. He was born in Bethlehem, not in Galilee. Further, He came from Heaven, but they denied it. They themselves fulfilled the prophecy of which they spoke. Nonetheless, Jesus said they did know. How was this so? The Holy Spirit testified to them who Jesus was. They could deny that they heard the Spirit's proclamation, but they did hear it.

> *30They sought therefore to take him: and no man laid his hand on him, because his hour was not yet come. 31But of the multitude many believed on him; and they said, When the Christ shall come, will he do more signs than those which this man hath done? 32The Pharisees heard the multitude murmuring*

*these things concerning him; and the chief priests and
the Pharisees sent officers to take him. 33Jesus therefore said, Yet a little while am I with you, and I go
unto him that sent me. 34Ye shall seek me, and shall
not find me: and where I am, ye cannot come. 35The
Jews therefore said among themselves, Whither will
this man go that we shall not find him? will he go
unto the Dispersion among the Greeks, and teach the
Greeks? 36What is this word that he said, Ye shall
seek me, and shall not find me; and where I am, ye
cannot come?*

What was so confusing to the guards and leaders about
Jesus' statements, "You will search for me and not find
me," and "You cannot go where I am going?" (NLT.) Jesus spoke these words not to the leaders directly, but to
the guards who came to arrest Him.   The guards would
have understood it in terms of their orders to arrest Him
– they thought He was telling them they wouldn't be able
to find Him to arrest Him. When the guards retold the
story to the chief priests, the priests put the statements
into a different context and thought perhaps He would
leave Jerusalem and go preach to the Greeks – an unwit-
ting and miraculous prophecy from the priests regarding
the future work of the Holy Spirit. They failed to grasp the
significance of what they were saying, and they failed to
grasp the role they were playing in bringing the prophecy
to fruition. Providence called upon them to play a pivotal
role in the unfolding of the mystery of the ages.

*37Now on the last day, the great day of the feast, Je-
sus stood and cried, saying, If any man thirst, let him
come unto me and drink.*

How was Jesus speaking when He "cried?" The term must signify the loud voice people use to be heard in unamplified settings. He was inviting everyone.

> *38He that believeth on me, as the scripture hath said, from within him shall flow rivers of living water. 39But this spake he of the Spirit, which they that believed on him were to receive: for the Spirit was not yet given; because Jesus was not yet glorified. 40Some of the multitude therefore, when they heard these words, said, This is of a truth the prophet. 41Others said, This is the Christ. But some said, What, doth the Christ come out of Galilee? 42Hath not the scripture said that the Christ cometh of the seed of David, and from Bethlehem, the village where David was? 43So there arose a division in the multitude because of him. 44And some of them would have taken him; but no man laid hands on him.*

The Gospel of John never says where Jesus was born, yet John mentions the ironic fact that many refused to believe in Jesus because they thought He was not born in Bethlehem and was not from the line of David. How often do I see something with my own eyes, but argue its reality away with my faulty logic based on my flawed assumptions? We know that sometimes evaluating what we see methodically and logically will save us from serious error. How do you know when to believe your eyes and when to believe your head? When the Holy Spirit, who is neither your eyes nor your head, convicts you, then you know. When He has done His work, your eyes and your head will align beautifully.

45 The officers therefore came to the chief priests and Pharisees; and they said unto them, Why did ye not bring him? 46 The officers answered, Never man so spake. 47 The Pharisees therefore answered them, Are ye also led astray?

" 'We have never heard anyone speak like this!' " (NLT.) The guards recognized the power of God, when the chief priests refused to. Each guard then had a choice, accept your King or keep taking your paycheck. I wonder how many of them eventually became followers of Jesus.

48 Hath any of the rulers believed on him, or of the Pharisees? 49 But this multitude that knoweth not the law are accursed.

How incredible that the leaders of the people could have such contempt for those whom the Lord had given into their care!

50 Nicodemus saith unto them (he that came to him before, being one of them), 51 Doth our law judge a man, except it first hear from himself and know what he doeth? 52 They answered and said unto him, Art thou also of Galilee? Search, and see that out of Galilee ariseth no prophet.

Nicodemus spoke up, perhaps timidly, in Jesus' defense. Did he make a lie of the leaders' claim that no ruler believed Jesus? He was not ready to forsake his heritage, as he saw it, nor was he able to completely deny Jesus – if only Jesus would defend Himself, he must have thought. It took courage to make even a half-hearted defense of Jesus against the Jewish rulers, and Nicodemus did not (yet) have the Holy Spirit living in him.

<u>The message of Chapter 7 applied to my life: Life is complicated, but the choice is simple</u>. Jesus' brothers saw Him through the eyes of jealousy. But jealousy is a sin; so to absolve themselves of guilt they manufactured a false conception of Him, one that made Him the defective one and left them feeling justified in their contempt. The people felt minimal commitment and minimal responsibility. They were there to hear what people like Jesus had to say, but they felt free to form their opinions and pass judgment without deep reflection or soul searching. They were basically an audience, there to be entertained. The guards were like the people in their passive acceptance of the status quo. They got paid to enforce the status quo, not to evaluate it. The fact their livelihood depended on supporting the status quo made them inclined to accept it as worthy. But they also had been inculcated with the scriptural values their leaders taught, so they recognized the power of Jesus' teachings. How could Jesus be right and their leaders be wrong? Yet what Jesus was saying had the ring of truth to it. They went back to their leaders for further guidance. The leaders were not unlike Jesus' brothers. They were so committed to holding on to their exalted positions in society that they willfully ignored the truth about Jesus. They manufactured a false narrative of what Jesus was saying, ignoring the clear conformity of His words to their own scriptures, so that they could despise Jesus and continue to exalt themselves. Then there was poor Nicodemus, the one leader who discerned the conflict between his allegiance to his social class and his love of God and the truth. What would he choose? Your class, your tribe, your society are powerful forces in the

here and now, pressuring you to conform. But when you know they are wrong, that God is presenting you with the opportunity to embrace Him and the truth, what do you do? If only God would take over the situation and make the choice easy (and thus cost free)!

53[And they went every man unto his own house:

Chapter 8: Jesus and the woman caught in adultery: Jesus came to save sinners. (Should we feel, "I am chief?")

Newer translations leave this story out of John because it is not in the oldest version of the book. That it was inserted in a later edition does not make it untrue. What would make us think that John spoke the gospel story one time and then never returned to it? He said himself that Jesus did so many things in His life on Earth that all the books in the world could not contain them. This incident adds something important to the narrative of Jesus' life that the author or compiler of John might have thought important enough to add to Jesus' biography later. There might, for instance have been a controversy in the church that made Jesus' teaching on forgiving the adulteress important. Here we see how forgiveness plays out in a restored and changed life. Forgiveness has real life consequences. This incident fits here, even though the narrative also flows well without it.

On this occasion, having been let down by the guards they had sent, the leaders go to Jesus themselves. They will prove His knowledge and political savvy cannot match their own. They will humiliate Jesus in front of everyone.

John 8 (ASV) 1but Jesus went unto the mount of Olives.

Because He had no house.

> *2And early in the morning he came again into the temple, and all the people came unto him; and he sat down, and taught them.*

The people were watching this drama play out between Jesus and the Pharisees.

> *3And the scribes and the Pharisees bring a woman taken in adultery; and having set her in the midst, 4they say unto him, Teacher, this woman hath been taken in adultery, in the very act. 5Now in the law Moses commanded us to stone such: what then sayest thou of her? 6And this they said, trying him, that they might have whereof to accuse him. But Jesus stooped down, and with his finger wrote on the ground.*

Did He write something important, or was He just letting the tension build? Could others see what He wrote? Stooping, writing in the sand, lifting himself back up, are not typical of John's descriptions of Jesus' behavior. These references make the story sound more like a personal recollection, recorded later.

> *7But when they continued asking him, he lifted up himself, and said unto them, He that is without sin among you, let him first cast a stone at her. 8And again he stooped down, and with his finger wrote on the ground. 9And they, when they heard it, went out one by one, beginning from the eldest, even unto the last: and Jesus was left alone, and the woman, where she was, in the midst.*

The people watching probably remained after the scribes and Pharisees had left, so they saw the resolution of the woman's story.

10And Jesus lifted up himself, and said unto her, Woman, where are they? did no man condemn thee? 11And she said, No man, Lord. And Jesus said, Neither do I condemn thee: go thy way; from henceforth sin no more.]

"Neither do I. Go and sin no more." (NLT.) What does Jesus mean? He is not absolving her of responsibility in the matter, but He is giving her another chance.

When Jesus gave her accusers permission to stone the woman, He indicted them without endangering her. They had thought of the damage He would cause Himself if He promoted the stoning, since it was unlawful under Roman law, but they had not anticipated His suggesting they carry out the stoning themselves. Even if they were willing to assert they had never sinned, they were too spineless to take on Roman authority by breaking Roman law. They fell into the very trap they had set for Jesus. And because He had linked their not stoning her with admission of their own culpability, He achieved His point that all were sinners, deserving punishment, and in part responsible for this woman's plight.

Why would it have been wrong to stone the woman for the sin of adultery? For the reason Jesus gave. The chain of sins in society that led to this woman's sin had gone unpunished. A society that allowed the mistreatment of wives, the casting off and neglect of those in need, offering contempt rather than loving care, all the engrained and accepted sinful attitudes and practices of Jewish society led up to this woman's sin. The very fact that for her to have been caught in the act of adultery meant that the man had been caught and excused of responsibility, demonstrated that the woman was the scapegoat, the victim of a sick society's inability to deal with its own inner corruption. Who are the scapegoats in our society?

Preview: Verses 12-29 seem to be circular arguing between Jesus and the Pharisaic unbelieving and supposedly believing Jews about who Jesus is. Even the "believing people" will not believe He is the "I AM." Is Jesus engaging in circular arguments? These are hard verses to put together.

> 12Again therefore Jesus spake unto them, saying, I am the light of the world: he that followeth me shall not walk in the darkness, but shall have the light of life.

To whom did Jesus speak these words? He had sent the woman away. Was He speaking to the observers who had watched the scene with the leaders and the woman unfold? Or was "again" the beginning of a different occasion? "Again" signifies a different occasion. Jesus is in another argument with the Pharisees. But for certain, Jesus spoke these words to me. Jesus, You are the light of the world. You have invited me to follow You, and I will never be lost in darkness.

> 13The Pharisees therefore said unto him, Thou bearest witness of thyself; thy witness is not true. 14Jesus answered and said unto them, Even if I bear witness of myself, my witness is true; for I know whence I came, and whither I go; but ye know not whence I come, or whither I go.

The Pharisees challenge Jesus' authority to make this claim of being the light of the world by putting Him in the position not of an authority, but of a witness at a trial. How do I regard Jesus, as my authority for life, or as a candidate who must prove Himself to me? Jesus claims authority. He has no need of supporting testimony. (It is noteworthy that this first set of detractors give Jesus the respect of including Him in the framework of their own, rabbinical style of reasoning. The next set of detractors do not.)

15Ye judge after the flesh; I judge no man.

What does Jesus mean, "I do not judge anyone."? (NLT.) Does He simply mean that He did not come to judge, but to rescue? To point out the truth about human depravity and need? "You judge me by human standards, but I do not judge anyone" (NLT), means: You are judging Me according to your logic and world view, not according to the Spirit. I do not judge anyone by your standards; I operate under the Father's direction, ...

16Yea and if I judge, my judgment is true; for I am not alone, but I and the Father that sent me.

but if I (Jesus) did apply logic and the information provided by the world, I would do it accurately, My judgment would not be distorted by sin. God the Father would be with Me in My judgment; in My experience, flesh and Spirit work together, as the Father originally intended.

17Yea and in your law it is written, that the witness of two men is true. 18I am he that beareth witness of myself, and the Father that sent me beareth witness of me. 19They said therefore unto him, Where is thy Father? Jesus answered, Ye know neither me, nor my Father: if ye knew me, ye would know my Father also.

Why does Jesus say, "in your law?" Because Mosaic law applies to the Jews. It does not apply to God.

Jesus spoke of the Father as an active reality in His experience. When the Pharisees tried to sidetrack the conversation by questioning who His father was, He brought them back to the point immediately. They are the ones who are blind to the truth and unable to judge reality, even though they are Israel's assigned judges. They are trapped in their own carnal thought processes.

> 20These words spake he in the treasury, as he taught in the temple: and no man took him; because his hour was not yet come.

> 21He said therefore again unto them, I go away, and ye shall seek me, and shall die in your sin: whither I go, ye cannot come. 22The Jews therefore said, Will he kill himself, that he saith, Whither I go, ye cannot come? 23And he said unto them, Ye are from beneath; I am from above: ye are of this world; I am not of this world. 24I said therefore unto you, that ye shall die in your sins: for except ye believe that I am he, ye shall die in your sins. 25They said therefore unto him, Who art thou?

"Who art thou?" How tragic for them and for Jesus. He is ready to die for them, but they are trapped within the confines of their spiritually warped world view. "Who art thou?" They are confused by choice.

> Jesus said unto them, Even that which I have also spoken unto you from the beginning. 26I have many things to speak and to judge concerning you: howbeit he that sent me is true; and the things which I heard from him, these speak I unto the world.

Jesus had many things to tell these people, but He was on His Father's timetable. What He said and did, and what He left unsaid and undone, were according to His Father's will.

> *27They perceived not that he spake to them of the Father. 28Jesus therefore said, When ye have lifted up the Son of man, then shall ye know that I am he, and that I do nothing of myself, but as the Father taught me, I speak these things.*

This generation of Jewish leaders will know the truth – that they killed God. But they still will not repent. Later generations inherited the lie these leaders handed down to them.

> *29And he that sent me is with me; he hath not left me alone; for I do always the things that are pleasing to him. 30As he spake these things, many believed on him.*

God prolonged this moment, keeping Jesus from arrest, so He could finish the conversation. He told them plainly, "you will die in your sins" (NLT), but they continued to regard the deficiency as being in Jesus and not in themselves. Jesus refrained from too detailed a recounting of their sin—it would only have made them more defensive. Instead He told them who He was by describing His relationship with the Father. Why did that cause some of them to accept His word (though not for long)? Did they see that He lived His life before the Father, conscience clear and devoted to Him?

> *31Jesus therefore said to those Jews that had believed him, If ye abide in my word, then are ye truly my dis-*

ciples; 32and ye shall know the truth, and the truth shall make you free.

This set of Jews has a different barrier to faith than the previous set Jesus addressed. What is it?

33They answered unto him, We are Abraham's seed, and have never yet been in bondage to any man: how sayest thou, Ye shall be made free? 34Jesus answered them, Verily, verily, I say unto you, Every one that committeth sin is the bondservant of sin. 35And the bondservant abideth not in the house for ever: the Son abideth for ever. 36If therefore the Son shall make you free, ye shall be free indeed. 37I know that ye are Abraham's seed: yet ye seek to kill me, because my word hath not free course in you. 38I speak the things which I have seen with my Father: and ye also do the things which ye heard from your father. 39They answered and said unto him, Our father is Abraham. Jesus saith unto them, If ye were Abraham's children, ye would do the works of Abraham. 40But now ye seek to kill me, a man that hath told you the truth, which I heard from God: this did not Abraham. 41Ye do the works of your father. They said unto him, We were not born of fornication; we have one Father, even God.

Jesus is telling them: It is not enough to be a physical descendant of Abraham. To be a child of Abraham you must commit yourself to Me. These men believed their inherited status as Jews preserved them from judgment. They were blind to their depravity in the eyes of God. These Jews claimed Abraham as their father. They claimed God as their Father. Jesus identified their father as the devil.

The devil is the "father" of those who set themselves up against God. These people, who had the Scripture, refused to apply its truths to themselves. Many "Christians" throughout the ages have faced the same temptation.

> *42Jesus said unto them, If God were your Father, ye would love me: for I came forth and am come from God; for neither have I come of myself, but he sent me. 43Why do ye not understand my speech? Even because ye cannot hear my word.*

Jesus and these Jews existed in different "realities." The truth of God did not penetrate their thought-world. From that day to this day the world has been full of such people. How and why it is so is a mystery in God's Providence.

> *44Ye are of your father the devil, and the lusts of your father it is your will to do. He was a murderer from the beginning, and standeth not in the truth, because there is no truth in him. When he speaketh a lie, he speaketh of his own: for he is a liar, and the father thereof. 45But because I say the truth, ye believe me not. 46Which of you convicteth me of sin? If I say truth, why do ye not believe me? 47He that is of God heareth the words of God: for this cause ye hear them not, because ye are not of God. 48The Jews answered and said unto him, Say we not well that thou art a Samaritan, and hast a demon?*

The worst insult they could think of was to call Jesus a Samaritan – a non-Jew. They misapprehended the truth that, "Salvation is from the Jews." God would turn these Jews' world upside down in order to make it so.

> *49Jesus answered, I have not a demon; but I honor my Father, and ye dishonor me. 50But I seek not mine own*

glory: there is one that seeketh and judgeth. 51Verily, verily, I say unto you, If a man keep my word, he shall never see death. 52The Jews said unto him, Now we know that thou hast a demon. Abraham died, and the prophets; and thou sayest, If a man keep my word, he shall never taste of death. 53Art thou greater than our father Abraham, who died? and the prophets died: whom makest thou thyself? 54Jesus answered, If I glorify myself, my glory is nothing: it is my Father that glorifieth me; of whom ye say, that he is your God; 55and ye have not known him: but I know him; and if I should say, I know him not, I shall be like unto you, a liar: but I know him, and keep his word.

Jesus' accusation is that they who claim to be descendants of Abraham and therefore in a special relationship with God are denying God when they deny Jesus. They have betrayed the true virtue in their heritage – faith in God.

56Your father Abraham rejoiced to see my day; and he saw it, and was glad. 57The Jews therefore said unto him, Thou art not yet fifty years old, and hast thou seen Abraham? 58Jesus said unto them, Verily, verily, I say unto you, Before Abraham was born, I am. 59They took up stones therefore to cast at him: but Jesus hid himself, and went out of the temple.

What a horrible time this must have been for Jesus. Unlike everyone else there, He understood the full import of this confrontation, and how it would end.

Those who superficially accepted Jesus, because they thought it put them a cut above those who were clearly condemned, still had to face the challenge He posed to them—they had to submit to Him their most cherished conceptions of themselves as superior beings. They had to accept that they were sinners in need of a Savior. Jesus knew these people would not do that. He knew they would reject Him in order to preserve their fake identities. They would perish rather than accept the truth about themselves.

Jesus said in verse 28 that when they crucified Him, then they would realize who He was. So, even then they would have a chance to repent and accept Him – which many did at Pentecost. And those such as Caiaphas, who kept on denying Him, knew whose side they were on – they had sided with the Devil.

In the final conversation, verses 31-59, Jesus took the argument against the self-righteousness of the Jews to its logical conclusion. He showed them the truth about themselves. Rather than repent in shame, they took up stones to kill Him. Lord, keep me ever repentant and never defensively self-righteous!

Chapter 9: Healing the man born blind. Do you see the Savior?

How long after the Temple confrontation was this incident? It could not have been immediately after, but it must not have been too long after it, either. Jesus as the light of the world is still the subject.

> *John 9 (ASV) 1And as he passed by, he saw a man blind from his birth. 2And his disciples asked him, saying, Rabbi, who sinned, this man, or his parents, that he should be born blind? 3Jesus answered, Neither did this man sin, nor his parents: but that the works of God should be made manifest in him.*

Sometimes we suffer so that God can be glorified. Yes, we sin, but the purpose of the suffering is not just discipline or retribution, it is so God can be glorified. God is glorified when His true nature and character are exhibited and understood. When God is glorified, good things happen!

Jesus explains the mystery of our lives being tied up in Providence. This man's blindness, at this particular moment in redemptive history, is an essential part of God's plan for the Jewish nation and the salvation of the world – but it is also a crucial part of the man's own salvation. Jesus turns what seemed a curse on the man into a blessing.

> *4We must work the works of him that sent me, while it is day: the night cometh, when no man can work.*

5When I am in the world, I am the light of the world.

What does Jesus mean that they must act quickly? Obedience must be immediate, in accordance with God's timetable, not our own. How tempting it is to procrastinate in our obedience. We want credit for obeying, but the luxury of choosing how soon. God does not give us this luxury! "The night is coming, and then no one can work." (NLT.) I think Jesus means the night that is about to fall on the Jewish nation. There will be no great revival work of the Holy Spirit among the Jews during "the times of the Gentiles" (Luke 21:24). Jesus had to fulfill God's plan for the Jewish nation during His lifetime on earth. After the cross, it would be too late. Jews would still come to Jesus and be born again and be filled with the Holy Spirit, but the time of the Jewish nation's special relationship with God in His plan of redemption would be over. Jesus is the light of the world, to the Jew and the Gentile. Without Jesus, there is no light. The Jewish nation chose to reject the light, to be blind, to live in darkness.

> *6When he had thus spoken, he spat on the ground, and made clay of the spittle, and anointed his eyes with the clay, 7and said unto him, Go, wash in the pool of Siloam (which is by interpretation, Sent). He went away therefore, and washed, and came seeing.*

This man did not ask for healing, as far as the passage describes, but he obeyed. He submitted himself to Jesus' healing actions and then he washed in the pool of Siloam. Were the man's eyes open or shut when Jesus put the mud on? Jesus formed new "eyes" out of the mud, to create what was missing in the eyes of one born blind.

8The neighbors therefore, and they that saw him aforetime, that he was a beggar, said, Is not this he that sat and begged? 9Others said, It is he: others said, No, but he is like him. He said, I am he. 10They said therefore unto him, How then were thine eyes opened? 11He answered, The man that is called Jesus made clay, and anointed mine eyes, and said unto me, Go to Siloam, and wash: so I went away and washed, and I received sight. 12And they said unto him, Where is he? He saith, I know not.

13They bring to the Pharisees him that aforetime was blind. 14Now it was the sabbath on the day when Jesus made the clay, and opened his eyes. 15Again therefore the Pharisees also asked him how he received his sight. And he said unto them, He put clay upon mine eyes, and I washed, and I see. 16Some therefore of the Pharisees said, This man is not from God, because he keepeth not the sabbath. But others said, How can a man that is a sinner do such signs? And there was division among them.

"A sinner" to these Jewish leaders meant a person they had designated as a sinner. They did not regard themselves as sinners. The only question was, in which category should they place Jesus, based on the evidence? Was He a sinner or was He one of them? Jesus would not allow Himself to be placed in the same category as they placed themselves. So, He had to be a sinner. Did any of them doubt their authority to make that judgment?

17They say therefore unto the blind man again, What sayest thou of him, in that he opened thine eyes?

If they were reduced to asking the opinion of the blind man, a known "sinner," they were at a complete loss. They were searching for grounds to condemn Jesus and having trouble finding them.

> *And he said, He is a prophet. 18The Jews therefore did not believe concerning him, that he had been blind, and had received his sight, until they called the parents of him that had received his sight, 19and asked them, saying, Is this your son, who ye say was born blind? How then doth he now see? 20His parents answered and said, We know that this is our son, and that he was born blind: 21but how he now seeth, we know not; or who opened his eyes, we know not: ask him; he is of age; he shall speak for himself. 22These things said his parents, because they feared the Jews: for the Jews had agreed already, that if any man should confess him to be Christ, he should be put out of the synagogue. 23Therefore said his parents, He is of age; ask him.*

Were his parents abandoning their son, or were they reacting in confusion and fear, hoping things would work out?

> *24So they called a second time the man that was blind, and said unto him, Give glory to God: we know that this man is a sinner. 25He therefore answered, Whether he is a sinner, I know not: one thing I know, that, whereas I was blind, now I see.*

The man's testimony only went as far as what he personally knew and had experienced. No one should testify beyond what they know personally to be true.

26They said therefore unto him, What did he to thee? How opened he thine eyes? 27He answered them, I told you even now, and ye did not hear; wherefore would ye hear it again? would ye also become his disciples?

Was he a smart aleck or was he pointing out that they already knew the two choices before them: deny the truth or follow Jesus?

28And they reviled him, and said, Thou art his disciple; but we are disciples of Moses. 29We know that God hath spoken unto Moses: but as for this man, we know not whence he is. 30The man answered and said unto them, Why, herein is the marvel, that ye know not whence he is, and yet he opened mine eyes. 31We know that God heareth not sinners: but if any man be a worshipper of God, and do his will, him he heareth. 32Since the world began it was never heard that any one opened the eyes of a man born blind. 33If this man were not from God, he could do nothing.

What a contrast between this man and the cripple Jesus had healed at Bethesda!

34They answered and said unto him, Thou wast altogether born in sins, and dost thou teach us? And they cast him out.

They judged the man to be a sinner from birth. How did they distinguish his prenatal situation from their own? Were they not also born in sin?

35Jesus heard that they had cast him out; and finding him, he said, Dost thou believe on the Son of God? 36He answered and said, And who is he, Lord, that I may believe on him? 37Jesus said unto him, Thou hast both seen him, and he it is that speaketh with thee. 38And he said, Lord, I believe. And he worshipped him.

The man was waiting for Jesus to reveal the truth to him. When he heard it, he accepted it. Would that I were always so ready!

39And Jesus said, For judgment came I into this world, that they that see not may see; and that they that see may become blind. 40Those of the Pharisees who were with him heard these things,

Why were these Pharisees "with" Jesus at this point? Were these the ones who were still undecided as to whether Jesus was a sinner?

and said unto him, Are we also blind? 41Jesus said unto them, If ye were blind, ye would have no sin: but now ye say, We see: your sin remaineth.

Jesus didn't judge them; they judged themselves by the decision they made. We are not condemned for what we do not know, but for how we respond to what we do know.

The man born blind only testified as to what he personally experienced, but it got him excommunicated from Jewish life. He is one of the first to suffer for his witness concerning Jesus. Circumstances beyond his control brought him to the moment when Jesus offered him a choice. And he chose Jesus. He was healed and forgiven.

The Pharisees received the same opportunity to believe. In verse 38 Jesus said He entered the world "for judgment" (ASV) or to "render judgment" (NLT), to give sight to the blind and to demonstrate that those who think they see are blind. How could He "judge no one" and yet "render judgment"? The judgment comes in the response to Jesus. He did not come to judge sinners in their present condition on their lives' journeys. That judgment had already been made. He came to offer us a way out from under that judgment.

Jesus offers you a mirror. Your response to what you see in the mirror – your judgment of yourself – determines your fate. Do you see yourself as a sinner in need of a Savior? Or do you insist that you are pure and that the defect is in anyone who challenges your status? When you get down to it, you are one or the other of these two kinds of people.

Chapter 10: The Light of Truth and Life is also my Shepherd. My Shepherd is One with the Father.

John 10 (ASV) 1Verily, verily, I say unto you, He that entereth not by the door into the fold of the sheep, but climbeth up some other way, the same is a thief and a robber. 2But he that entereth in by the door is the shepherd of the sheep. 3To him the porter openeth; and the sheep hear his voice: and he calleth his own sheep by name, and leadeth them out. 4When he hath put forth all his own, he goeth before them, and the sheep follow him: for they know his voice. 5And a stranger will they not follow, but will flee from him: for they know not the voice of strangers. 6This parable spake Jesus unto them: but they understood not what things they were which he spake unto them.

Jesus is describing the course of history future. If you belong to Jesus, you will recognize His voice and you will follow Him. Even if you are far off and never heard about Him, when Jesus calls, then you will follow. What about those attracted to false religions? Is it too late for them? No. The sheep are waiting to hear their Shepherd's voice. If they have never heard it, they may be confused for a time by an imposter and think, "This is the Shepherd," but when the true Shepherd calls, then they will know and they will follow.

7Jesus therefore said unto them again, Verily, verily, I say unto you, I am the door of the sheep. 8All that came before me are thieves and robbers: but the sheep did not hear them.

Who were these "thieves and robbers?" Were there many false messiahs leading up to Jesus? Knowing that something was stirring in Providence, did Satan raise up false teachers and messiahs to lead people away from the truth? Or were these "thieves and robbers" the religious leaders who claimed to know and teach the way to God when they actually knew nothing of the truth? Jesus is not talking about those who came before Him and pointed to Him, but to those who claimed to be Him (to have God's authority).

9I am the door; by me if any man enter in, he shall be saved, and shall go in and go out, and shall find pasture. 10The thief cometh not, but that he may steal, and kill, and destroy: I came that they may have life, and may have it abundantly. 11I am the good shepherd: the good shepherd layeth down his life for the sheep. 12He that is a hireling, and not a shepherd, whose own the sheep are not, beholdeth the wolf coming, and leaveth the sheep, and fleeth, and the wolf snatcheth them, and scattereth them: 13he fleeth because he is a hireling, and careth not for the sheep.

Who are the "hirelings?" Surely these include the religious leaders of the time, appointed to preserve the people until the Shepherd came, but who cared not for the people, but only for their own exalted positions. Doesn't it also include the church leaders of all times, who use their positions in the church to further their personal ambitions, and ignore the needs of Christ's people?

14I am the good shepherd; and I know mine own, and mine own know me, 15even as the Father knoweth me, and I know the Father; and I lay down my life for the sheep. 16And other sheep I have, which are not of this fold: them also I must bring, and they shall hear my voice: and they shall become one flock, one shepherd. 17Therefore doth the Father love me, because I lay down my life, that I may take it again. 18No one taketh it away from me, but I lay it down of myself. I have power to lay it down, and I have power to take it again. This commandment received I from my Father.

I don't know anything about sheep and shepherds, but Jesus' description of our relationship is such a comfort! I am one of the sheep from another sheepfold that Jesus has gathered to Himself. At what a cost! He laid down His life for His sheep, for me. Not in an emergency. It was part of His pre-determined plan with the Father.

19There arose a division again among the Jews because of these words. 20And many of them said, He hath a demon, and is mad; why hear ye him? 21Others said, These are not the sayings of one possessed with a demon. Can a demon open the eyes of the blind?

Jesus' miracles had earned Him a hearing. How sad that some of the scholars of the past couple hundred years have sought to remove miracles from the gospel. The average person today knows, as did the average person of 30 AD, that it is the miracles that witness to the authenticity of the Jesus' message. The Holy Spirit witnesses to our hearts and the miracles witness to our eyes and minds. In combination, the two witnesses are conclusive.

> *22And it was the feast of the dedication at Jerusalem: 23it was winter; and Jesus was walking in the temple in Solomon's porch. 24The Jews therefore came round about him, and said unto him, How long dost thou hold us in suspense? If thou art the Christ, tell us plainly. 25Jesus answered them, I told you, and ye believe not: the works that I do in my Father's name, these bear witness of me. 26But ye believe not, because ye are not of my sheep. 27My sheep hear my voice, and I know them, and they follow me: 28and I give unto them eternal life; and they shall never perish, and no one shall snatch them out of my hand. 29My Father, who hath given them unto me, is greater than all; and no one is able to snatch them out of the Father's hand. 30I and the Father are one. 31The Jews took up stones again to stone him.*

They wanted Him to declare Himself, complained that He hadn't, and when He did, they wanted to kill Him. They wanted Him to declare Himself so they could justify killing Him.

> *32Jesus answered them, Many good works have I showed you from the Father; for which of those works do ye stone me? 33The Jews answered him, For a good work we stone thee not, but for blasphemy; and because that thou, being a man, makest thyself God. 34Jesus answered them, Is it not written in your law, I said, ye are gods? 35If he called them gods, unto whom the word of God came (and the scripture cannot be*

broken), 36say ye of him, whom the Father sanctified and sent into the world, Thou blasphemest; because I said, I am the Son of God? 37If I do not the works of my Father, believe me not. 38But if I do them, though ye believe not me, believe the works: that ye may know and understand that the Father is in me, and I in the Father. 39They sought again to take him: and he went forth out of their hand.

Jesus was, as He said, present in the Old Testament Scriptures. He was not a new thing. He was always there, but was now being revealed in a new and clearer light. Some complain that Jesus should have declared who He was at the very beginning of His ministry. Instead He revealed Himself by His words and His miracles, adding one layer of the reality of who he was upon another, so that those experiencing it could adjust to it and those looking back on it could understand how He fit into the whole story of mankind and the history of salvation.

40And he went away again beyond the Jordan into the place where John was at the first baptizing; and there be abode. 41And many came unto him; and they said, John indeed did no sign: but all things whatsoever John spake of this man were true. 42And many believed on him there.

John had not performed any miracles. But He had prophesied of Jesus the Messiah. Now in this time of controversy and doubt, John's testimony was bearing fruit. John's "sign" was the fulfillment of his prophecies about Jesus. Only those who live in the Kingdom can know the true grandeur of John the Baptist's message.

Events in Chapter 10 occur during Hanukkah. Jesus walked in the Temple. The leaders demanded He tell them whether He was the Messiah and He responded that He had already told them. They could not see it, because He is not meeting their expectations of the Messiah. He is the Messiah God had sent, but He was not the Messiah they wanted. He was doing God's work, but not the work they expected and wanted. Unwilling to change their expectations in the face of reality, they wanted to kill Him. Why? They could not see Jesus for who He is because they were not His sheep.

Jesus left Jerusalem for the spot where John baptized Him. Many among the people went with Him. They believed, because of His miracles – His miracles did indeed testify that God's seal of approval was on Him. But those who hated Him would not be swayed by any miracle. The only God they would recognize was one of their own making, who put their values and ambitions first. How many of us become angry and reject reality when it challenges our view of ourselves? Denying reality puts you on the wrong side of history, the truth, and God.

Chapter 11: The miracle that cannot be ignored: the raising of Lazarus.

> *John 11 (ASV) 1Now a certain man was sick, Lazarus of Bethany, of the village of Mary and her sister Martha. 2And it was that Mary who anointed the Lord with ointment, and wiped his feet with her hair, whose brother Lazarus was sick. 3The sisters therefore sent unto him, saying, Lord, behold, he whom thou lovest is sick.*

Why did they appeal to Jesus this way? Were they asking for special treatment, or just coming as needy and helpless beggars? They must have thought Jesus had a personal interest in Lazarus. When I need help I want to be confident that Jesus knows me personally and has a personal interest in my well-being. Jesus is all about relationships. Jesus healed strangers very readily, but that was because they weren't really strangers. As God of the Universe, He already had a relationship with each of them.

> *4But when Jesus heard it, he said, This sickness is not unto death, but for the glory of God, that the Son of God may be glorified thereby. 5Now Jesus loved Martha, and her sister, and Lazarus. 6When therefore he heard that he was sick, he abode at that time two days in the place where he was.*

We see here how God's personal love for us and His commitment to justice and the salvation of the world work together. Jesus gave Martha, Mary, and Lazarus the joy and honor of being part of the world's salvation story.

> *7Then after this he saith to the disciples, Let us go into Judaea again. 8The disciples say unto him, Rabbi, the Jews were but now seeking to stone thee; and goest thou thither again?*

Jesus' disciples cared more for his safety than for Lazarus. Where was their faith, their confidence in their Messiah?

> *9Jesus answered, Are there not twelve hours in the day? If a man walk in the day, he stumbleth not, because he seeth the light of this world.*

Obey God and your path is safe – it will be "day" for you.

> *10But if a man walk in the night, he stumbleth, because the light is not in him.*

"Night" is the darkness that comes to our understanding when we disobey the Father.

> *11These things spake he: and after this he saith unto them, Our friend Lazarus is fallen asleep; but I go, that I may awake him out of sleep. 12The disciples therefore said unto him, Lord, if he is fallen asleep, he will recover. 13Now Jesus had spoken of his death: but they thought that he spake of taking rest in sleep. 14Then Jesus therefore said unto them plainly, Lazarus is dead. 15And I am glad for your sakes that I was not there, to the intent ye may believe; nevertheless let us go unto him.*

Lazarus' death was part of God's plan. Jesus was all about following the Father's schedule.

16Thomas therefore, who is called Didymus, said unto his fellow-disciples, Let us also go, that we may die with him.

Jesus had a knowledge of the workings of God's Providence that we lack. He stayed away two days after the message of Lazarus' illness arrived, so that Lazarus would be dead and that His power and God's glory would be displayed and bring people to faith. Jesus knew that even His disciples needed convincing. Thomas loved Jesus, but he did not understand His power. Jesus controlled the moment and the future. He controlled His own destiny.

Introducing the raising of Lazarus. Mary and Martha are among the few women mentioned in the gospels, but John has a lot to say about them, compared with other personalities, male and female, in Jesus' life. Mary is remembered for sitting at Jesus' feet, for her conversation with Jesus when Lazarus had died, and for washing Jesus' feet with her hair. When she did this, she must have known that a prostitute had done it previously. In honoring Jesus this way, she humbled herself and identified with the weakest and most despised in society. She saw herself as being in the same position before God as that woman was – a sinner who loves her Savior.

17So when Jesus came, he found that he had been in the tomb four days already. 18Now Bethany was nigh unto Jerusalem, about fifteen furlongs off; 19and many of the Jews had come to Martha and Mary, to console them concerning their brother. 20Martha therefore, when she heard that Jesus was coming, went and met him: but Mary still sat in the house. 21Martha there-

fore said unto Jesus, Lord, if thou hadst been here, my
brother had not died. 22And even now I know that,
whatsoever thou shalt ask of God, God will give thee.

"But even now I know God will give You what You ask."
(NLT.) Martha expected Jesus to do something about the
situation. She knew He had come for that reason.

23Jesus saith unto her, Thy brother shall rise again.

When Jesus said "Your brother will rise again" (NLT) what
was He doing? He was starting Martha on the next step of
her faith journey. She was going to get to see her brother
rise that day – but for the rest of us, Jesus has promised we
will rise again too. Here He refers to physical resurrection.
In a minute He will refer to spiritual rebirth. He promises
Martha, and us, both.

24Martha saith unto him, I know that he shall rise
again in the resurrection at the last day.

How did she know this? Where do the Scriptures say it? I
don't think the Old Testament clearly taught a resurrection of the dead and a final judgment. Part of God's setting
the stage for the Incarnation was the wealth of post-Old
Testament writing circulating between 400 B.C. and Jesus'
coming. Was one of the benefits of the rabbis having 400
years to study the Old Testament before Jesus' birth that
some of them found the resurrection and hope of eternal
life within the Scriptures?

25Jesus said unto her, I am the resurrection, and the
life: he that believeth on me, though he die, yet shall
he live;   26and whosoever liveth and believeth on
me shall never die. Believest thou this? 27She saith

unto him, Yea, Lord: I have believed that thou art the Christ, the Son of God, even he that cometh into the world. 28And when she had said this, she went away, and called Mary her sister secretly, saying, The Teacher is here, and calleth thee. 29And she, when she heard it, arose quickly, and went unto him.

Why didn't Mary come to Jesus when Martha did? Because Mary didn't know Jesus had come. Why didn't Martha tell her? Perhaps because Martha knew that if she and Mary both left the house, the people would follow and she would not have an opportunity to speak to Jesus alone. Why did Jesus allow them to suffer so? He says why twice. In verses 15 and 42 He says He did it so that people would have the opportunity to believe He was who He said He was. That included Martha, Mary, and Lazarus.

How much did Martha really understand? She knew that Jesus could have healed Lazarus. She knew Jesus was the promised Messiah. She knew that at the end of the age all the dead would be resurrected. What didn't she know? That Jesus is the resurrection and the life, and those who believe in Him have already passed from spiritual death to spiritual life. Their physical death, whenever it happens, is just a mile marker in their progress through eternity with God the Son, God the Holy Spirit, and God the Father. When they die physically, they immediately join Jesus in Heaven, and when He resurrects their bodies, they will live with Jesus in their resurrection bodies in the City He has prepared for them to dwell with the Father.

30(Now Jesus was not yet come into the village, but was still in the place where Martha met him.) 31The

Jews then who were with her in the house, and were consoling her, when they saw Mary, that she rose up quickly and went out, followed her, supposing that she was going unto the tomb to weep there. 32Mary therefore, when she came where Jesus was, and saw him, fell down at his feet, saying unto him, Lord, if thou hadst been here, my brother had not died. 33When Jesus therefore saw her weeping, and the Jews also weeping who came with her, he groaned in the spirit, and was troubled, 34and said, Where have ye laid him? They say unto him, Lord, come and see. 35Jesus wept.

Why was Jesus so upset at Lazarus death? He could have prevented it. Here for a change, instead of being angry with hypocritical human beings, He seems angry with the fate they all suffer – death. Jesus didn't come just to defeat hypocrisy. He came to defeat death. Yet isn't death part of God's solution for our sinfulness? Don't we die because we are sinners and are denied the fruit of the Tree of Life? Is Jesus' anger directed in part at us because we are the ones who caused this whole debacle, which can only be salvaged by Jesus' death for us?

Lazarus' death is the consequence of God's judgment on Adam in Genesis 3. God placed the flaming sword to guard the Tree of Life from man. Yet all men approach, because all men want to live. Their access to paradise is blocked and instead of life they receive death. Jesus came to remove the flaming sword so that we could enter into paradise with Him – but the sacrifice He had to make to achieve that for us was worthy of His anger. He wasn't angry with the Father for our fate. He was angry with us – we were to blame – even though He loved us and was willing to make the sacrifice. Is the "flaming sword" the certainty of death?

> *36The Jews therefore said, Behold how he loved him! 37But some of them said, Could not this man, who opened the eyes of him that was blind, have caused that this man also should not die? 38Jesus therefore again groaning in himself cometh to the tomb. Now it was a cave, and a stone lay against it. 39Jesus saith, Take ye away the stone. Martha, the sister of him that was dead, saith unto him, Lord, by this time the body decayeth; for he hath been dead four days. 40Jesus saith unto her, Said I not unto thee, that, if thou believedst, thou shouldest see the glory of God? 41So they took away the stone.*

They didn't expect a miracle, but they responded to Jesus' confidence and authority.

> *And Jesus lifted up his eyes, and said, Father, I thank thee that thou heardest me. 42And I knew that thou hearest me always: but because of the multitude that standeth around I said it, that they may believe that thou didst send me.*

Jesus did a lot of explaining here. He wanted us to realize that what He did and said then was for our sake, so that we would understand what would otherwise be a silent transaction between Him and the Father.

> *43And when he had thus spoken, he cried with a loud voice, Lazarus, come forth. 44He that was dead came forth, bound hand and foot with grave-clothes; and his face was bound about with a napkin. Jesus saith unto them, Loose him, and let him go.*

The facts that Lazarus came out of the tomb in his grave clothes and that Jesus left His behind when He rose is important to our understanding of Jesus' resurrection (and our future one). Lazarus' dead cells were reconstituted as living physical cells. Jesus' cells were transformed into something different and new.

> *45Many therefore of the Jews, who came to Mary and beheld that which he did, believed on him.*

That Mary and Martha lived in Bethany, so close to Jerusalem was part of God's plan. (Is there a better definition of Providence than God's plan?)

The plot to kill Jesus:

> *46But some of them went away to the Pharisees, and told them the things which Jesus had done.*

Were they rats or were they looking for guidance from their spiritual leaders?

> *47The chief priests therefore and the Pharisees gathered a council, and said, What do we? for this man doeth many signs.*

The answer to their question seems obvious – give glory to God and go out to meet your Savior. But that isn't even a thought with them.

> *48If we let him thus alone, all men will believe on him: and the Romans will come and take away both our place and our nation.*

The leaders did not doubt Jesus' miraculous powers, but they clearly believed the Roman army was more powerful than Jesus. Where did they put God in this calculation?

Did they think God was with Jesus, but too weak to take on Rome? Did they think a man could perform miracles independent of God? It has to be one or the other. I think that in their hearts they had set themselves up to oppose God, but on a conscious level they had to provide an intellectual argument to justify their opposition to Jesus.

> *49But a certain one of them, Caiaphas, being high priest that year, said unto them, Ye know nothing at all, 50nor do ye take account that it is expedient for you that one man should die for the people, and that the whole nation perish not. 51Now this he said not of himself: but, being high priest that year, he prophesied that Jesus should die for the nation; 52and not for the nation only, but that he might also gather together into one the children of God that are scattered abroad.*

Caiaphas' prophecy. He called his fellows foolish because they would not make what he saw as the only logical decision, based on their ambitions. The decision was not to embrace the miracle-working Savior, but to kill Him. For Caiaphas, this assured he and his fellows would remain in power, though under the boot of Rome. This, for him, was salvation. The death of Jesus would save Caiaphas' lifestyle for another 40 years. How often do I embrace reality-defying conclusions in order to preserve a world view and lifestyle that I mistakenly believe serves my best interests? The truth, no matter how uncomfortable at the time, is better.

> *53So from that day forth they took counsel that they might put him to death.*

54Jesus therefore walked no more openly among the Jews, but departed thence into the country near to the wilderness, into a city called Ephraim; and there he tarried with the disciples. 55Now the passover of the Jews was at hand: and many went up to Jerusalem out of the country before the passover, to purify themselves. 56They sought therefore for Jesus, and spake one with another, as they stood in the temple, What think ye? That he will not come to the feast? 57Now the chief priests and the Pharisees had given commandment, that, if any man knew where he was, he should show it, that they might take him.

Jesus stayed in Ephraim until the Passover. Surely He was preparing His disciples. While the people speculated rather than taking a position for the truth, the leaders finally took a united stand in opposition to the truth – arrest Jesus. How often do I sit on the sidelines and speculate, when I already have enough information to take a stand?

Chapter 12: The Party; the Plot; Palm Sunday; Greeks seeking Jesus; what Jesus demands; Who will follow? (The forces of history converge on one life. Can Jesus the healer, Jesus the friend of sinners, defeat the forces of evil and reconcile the whole world to Himself?)

> *John 12 (ASV) 1Jesus therefore six days before the passover came to Bethany, where Lazarus was, whom Jesus raised from the dead. 2So they made him a supper there: and Martha served; but Lazarus was one of them that sat at meat with him. 3Mary therefore took a pound of ointment of pure nard, very precious, and anointed the feet of Jesus, and wiped his feet with her hair: and the house was filled with the odor of the ointment.*

Was this ointment left over from Lazarus' funeral?

> *4But Judas Iscariot, one of his disciples, that should betray him, saith, 5Why was not this ointment sold for three hundred shillings, and given to the poor? 6Now this he said, not because he cared for the poor; but because he was a thief, and having the bag took away what was put therein.*

Jesus came to Bethany, knowing His death was very near. Was it a joyful party or a sad one? What mood did Mary set by pouring the oil on Jesus and washing His feet? Judas definitely wasn't in the mood, whatever the mood was.

How often are my valid criticisms really motivated by jealousy or some other base emotion?

> *7Jesus therefore said, Suffer her to keep it against the day of my burying. 8For the poor ye have always with you; but me ye have not always.*

Jesus ignored Judas' base motives and answered the question. It is a question that frequently confronts Christians: how to prioritize giving. All giving is to God, but how much should be "practical" and how much extravagant worship? If you live in a world of limited resources, that is an important question. Let the Spirit give wisdom.

"You will always have the poor among you, but you will not always have me." (NLT.) Jesus cared for the poor, but He knew we humans only have limited resources and must prioritize our spending. Worship of the true God has a high priority. In His life on Earth, what did Jesus spend on His worship / fellowship with the Father? He could have been rich, but He gave all His time and effort to His relationship with the Father and His service to human beings, because of His love of the Father. I imagine He followed whatever the ritual prescriptions for offerings were, out of loving obedience, but nowhere do we see Him giving more material offerings than what was prescribed – no kingly display of worship by offering hundreds of rams .... He gave Himself, an extravagant sacrifice, and that was better than rams.

> *9The common people therefore of the Jews learned that he was there: and they came, not for Jesus' sake only, but that they might see Lazarus also, whom he*

had raised from the dead. 10But the chief priests took counsel that they might put Lazarus also to death; 11because that by reason of him many of the Jews went away, and believed on Jesus.

When we follow Jesus fully, we share His earthly fate.

12On the morrow

What is John's calendar of Holy Week? It appears that the Lazarus' party would have been after sundown on Saturday – thus part of the first day of the week by Jewish reckoning. "The morrow" would have been the morning of the same day (the first day of the week), Sunday morning to us. If six days elapsed until the Passover, Passover would have begun Friday evening (the beginning of the Sabbath to the Jews), and the day of Jesus' death as the Passover Lamb would have been Friday, when the lambs were slain in preparation for the Passover meal. The Last Supper would have been a substitute for the Passover meal that Jesus desired to eat with His disciples.

a great multitude that had come to the feast, when they heard that Jesus was coming to Jerusalem, 13took the branches of the palm trees, and went forth to meet him, and cried out, Hosanna: Blessed is he that cometh in the name of the Lord, even the King of Israel. 14And Jesus, having found a young ass, sat thereon; as it is written, 15Fear not, daughter of Zion: behold, thy King cometh, sitting on an ass's colt. 16These things understood not his disciples at the first: but when Jesus was glorified, then remembered they that these things were written of him, and that they had done these things unto him.

How often do I do things, or observe things, with no understanding of their significance to God and His plan? All the time. Open my eyes, Lord!

> *17The multitude therefore that was with him when he called Lazarus out of the tomb, and raised him from the dead, bare witness. 18For this cause also the multitude went and met him, for that they heard that he had done this sign. 19The Pharisees therefore said among themselves, Behold how ye prevail nothing: lo, the world is gone after him.*

Jesus had Jerusalem in the palm of His hand on Palm Sunday. The leaders admitted defeat; they could not stop Him. But He did not seize power. They must have wondered at His delay. Later it must have seemed providential to them that they were given the opportunity to kill Him – and it was!

> *20Now there were certain Greeks among those that went up to worship at the feast: 21these therefore came to Philip, who was of Bethsaida of Galilee, and asked him, saying, Sir, we would see Jesus. 22Philip cometh and telleth Andrew: Andrew cometh, and Philip, and they tell Jesus. 23And Jesus answereth them, saying, The hour is come, that the Son of man should be glorified. 24Verily, verily, I say unto you, Except a grain of wheat fall into the earth and die, it abideth by itself alone; but if it die, it beareth much fruit. 25He that loveth his life loseth it; and he that hateth his life in this world shall keep it unto life eternal.*

I have to learn this lesson daily. I am dead and my life is hid with Christ in God!

26If any man serve me, let him follow me; and where I am, there shall also my servant be: if any man serve me, him will the Father honor.

Greeks come to see Jesus – that was bold of them. But what made them think they would succeed in getting their audience? Perhaps they had come to Jerusalem with no idea of what was afoot. When they heard the Messiah was at hand, how excited they would have been! Jesus' reply to Phillip's and Andrew's request on behalf of the Greeks explains that He must die so that others, such as these Greeks, might live as part of the new human race – the Church. He lays the ground rules for those who would follow Him. They must care nothing for their own lives, they must follow Him. The Father will honor them, and they will keep their lives for eternity. Did these Greeks hear Jesus say this? Did they get to see Jesus? Or did Andrew and Phillip just convey the message to them? "[T]hey went together to ask Jesus" (NLT), given the situation, probably means that Andrew and Phillip took the Greeks with them, and thus the Greeks would have heard Jesus' reply. Jesus gave them the same opportunity that Jews had to be His disciples. He was about to die in order to make the opportunity available to them. Whether they became His disciples was up to them. He made it clear it was a hard choice, but one with a great reward – receiving honor from the Father. Jesus never asks us to do anything he hasn't done Himself.

27Now is my soul troubled; and what shall I say? Father, save me from this hour. But for this cause came I unto this hour. 28Father, glorify thy name. There came therefore a voice out of heaven, saying, I have

both glorified it, and will glorify it again. 29The mul-
titude therefore, that stood by, and heard it, said that
it had thundered: others said, An angel hath spoken
to him.

When the Father spoke from heaven, the Greeks would
have heard the Voice and would have known it was in response to Jesus' request that the Father's name be glorified. They had a ringside seat. The Father would be glorified in Jesus' obedience, death, and resurrection. By their
own words, men, and the power within them, the devil,
would be judged.

30Jesus answered and said, This voice hath not come
for my sake, but for your sakes.

Jesus often did things in a way that enabled onlookers to
grasp what was happening. His life was intended to show
people the way.

31Now is the judgment of this world: now shall the
prince of this world be cast out. 32And I, if I be lift-
ed up from the earth, will draw all men unto myself.
33But this he said, signifying by what manner of death
he should die.

Jesus knew He would be crucified and not stoned.

The occasion of the Greeks coming to Jesus became the
occasion of Jesus focusing on the horror and imminence
of His own death. He had to die in order to draw all men to
Himself. In Jesus' death would be reconciled the apparent
senselessness of human life and history with God's grand
plan of saving humans from the destruction they brought
(and continue bringing today) on themselves. Jesus, the

totally guiltless man, died either because reality is completely senseless, if not evil, or because God has a plan beyond our imaginings and Jesus purposely worked to fulfill it in every detail. Chaos or intricate plan? Scripture makes it clear.

> *34The multitude therefore answered him, We have heard out of the law that the Christ abideth for ever: and how sayest thou, The Son of man must be lifted up? who is this Son of man? 35Jesus therefore said unto them, Yet a little while is the light among you. Walk while ye have the light, that darkness overtake you not: and he that walketh in the darkness knoweth not whither he goeth. 36While ye have the light, believe on the light, that ye may become sons of light.*

You are not a son of the light until you believe in the light.

The Jewish crowd was still set on fitting Jesus into their tiny box of rabbinical orthodoxy. We are to test everything by Scripture – even our own self-centered, small-minded way of interpreting Scripture. Only Holy Spirit can explain Scripture to us! "Put your trust in the light while there is still time ...." (NLT.) The light was right in front of them – would they choose to see or choose to remain blind? How many people choose blindness without acknowledging the momentousness of their decision?

> *These things spake Jesus, and he departed and hid himself from them.*
>
> *37But though he had done so many signs before them, yet they believed not on him: 38that the word of Isaiah the prophet might be fulfilled, which he spake,*

Lord, who hath believed our report?

And to whom hath the arm of the Lord been revealed?

39For this cause they could not believe, for that Isaiah said again,

40He hath blinded their eyes, and he hardened their heart;

Lest they should see with their eyes, and perceive with their heart,

And should turn,

And I should heal them.

41These things said Isaiah because he saw his glory; and he spake of him. 42Nevertheless even of the rulers many believed on him; but because of the Pharisees they did not confess it, lest they should be put out of the synagogue: 43for they loved the glory that is of men more than the glory that is of God.

Even the peoples' blindness was part of God's plan. Faith came to whom it would come according to God's timing. Some believed then, but pretended to deny it, because they valued their status on Earth more than their status in Heaven. Some would believe later, at Pentecost and even after that. Oh the shame and guilt they must have experienced upon coming to faith and realizing the part they had played in the Lord's murder. But that too was part of God's plan. And existentially, I am as responsible as they. Do I experience the grief due to God for my role in the tragedy?

44And Jesus cried and said, He that believeth on me, believeth not on me, but on him that sent me. 45And he that beholdeth me beholdeth him that sent me. 46I am come a light into the world, that whosoever believeth on me may not abide in the darkness. 47And if any man hear my sayings, and keep them not, I judge him not: for I came not to judge the world, but to save the world. 48He that rejecteth me, and receiveth not my sayings, hath one that judgeth him: the word that I spake, the same shall judge him in the last day.

The truth of Jesus' claim is an independent reality. A truth that we can accept now or confront later; but it will not go away.

49For I spake not from myself; but the Father that sent me, he hath given me a commandment, what I should say, and what I should speak. 50And I know that his commandment is life eternal: the things therefore which I speak, even as the Father hath said unto me, so I speak.

Jesus' message of salvation: If you have seen Jesus, you have seen the Father – you can trust that what He says reflects the Father's nature and will for us. He came to save, not to judge; but those who refuse to be saved will inevitably face judgment – it is the only alternative to salvation. Believe Jesus and have eternal life. Your eternal destiny depends on your response to Jesus' claim that salvation is in Him alone, that He is God's Son, the Door to Heaven.

When did Jesus say this to the crowds? In verse 36 He left the confrontation with them and hid Himself. He must have said this before leaving them, and John added it to show Jesus gave them every opportunity to believe and avoid the fate assigned in Isaiah 53 and 6.

Jesus seemed to be a denial of everything the Jews believed about worshipping the one God by following carefully prescribed rituals throughout life. Jesus was saying, You followed that path while you were waiting for Me. It kept you safe until I arrived. But now I'm here. Now you can follow Me. I am your path. Stay on the old path and it will lead to destruction. The people couldn't handle the challenge Jesus posed. They couldn't give up the comfortable identity they had formed for themselves to take on the identity Jesus offered them. Can I? Jesus constantly challenges me: "Follow Me." "I am the light."

Chapter 13: The Last Supper; The Savior serves; the Savior confronts His betrayer.

John 13 (ASV) 1Now before the feast of the passover,

The Last Supper was not the Passover meal. It was an alternative to it – it was "before the feast," because Jesus Himself was to be sacrificed as the Passover Lamb, before the Passover, which began Friday evening (the beginning of Jewish Saturday). Jesus would have liked to eat the Passover meal with His disciples, He desired to do it, but He could not. The Father's plan was for Him to be the Passover.

> *Jesus knowing that his hour was come that he should depart out of this world unto his Father, having loved his own that were in the world, he loved them unto the end. 2And during supper, the devil having already put into the heart of Judas Iscariot, Simon's son, to betray him, 3Jesus, knowing that the Father had given all the things into his hands, and that he came forth from God, and goeth unto God, 4riseth from supper, and layeth aside his garments; and he took a towel, and girded himself.*

"Jesus knew that the Father had given Him authority over everything and that He had come from God and would return to God." (NLT.) So what did He do? He became a servant and He served. God humbled Himself out of love for His disciples.

5Then he poureth water into the basin, and began to wash the disciples' feet, and to wipe them with the towel wherewith he was girded. 6So he cometh to Simon Peter. He saith unto him, Lord, dost thou wash my feet? 7Jesus answered and said unto him, What I do thou knowest not now; but thou shalt understand hereafter. 8Peter saith unto him, Thou shalt never wash my feet. Jesus answered him, If I wash thee not, thou hast no part with me. 9Simon Peter saith unto him, Lord, not my feet only, but also my hands and my head. 10Jesus saith to him, He that is bathed needeth not save to wash his feet, but is clean every whit: and ye are clean, but not all. 11For he knew him that should betray him; therefore said he, Ye are not all clean.

Why did Peter resist being washed? Did Peter resist because he honored Jesus so much or because he was too proud to be an object lesson? If I had been Peter I would have resisted out of pride – I revered Jesus but I also based my own status on His – if He were lowly then I would be lowly as well.

Why did Jesus refuse to wash all of him? Peter was already saved. But he had some worldliness that needed to be washed away – his pride of status. In Peter's case, Jesus' object lesson served the underlying purpose of Jesus' servanthood ministry. God humbled Himself to save Peter from Peter.

What is the point of performing an act your audience doesn't understand? Even if the disciples didn't understand the meaning of the act, it had a huge impact on them, and over time it became more and more meaningful and significant to them.

Of all the event in Jesus' life, this Last Supper seems most clearly to have been enacted for the benefit of posterity. But in truth, it was so with every event in Jesus' life. Past, present, and future intersected at every moment of Jesus' life.

> *12So when he had washed their feet, and taken his garments, and sat down again, he said unto them, Know ye what I have done to you? 13Ye call me, Teacher, and, Lord: and ye say well; for so I am. 14If I then, the Lord and the Teacher, have washed your feet, ye also ought to wash one another's feet. 15For I have given you an example, that ye also should do as I have done to you. 16Verily, verily, I say unto you, a servant is not greater than his lord; neither one that is sent greater than he that sent him. 17If ye know these things, blessed are ye if ye do them.*

The disciples had the rest of their lives to ponder and apply what Jesus told them about servanthood. When a disciple washes another disciple's feet, he cleanses himself in the process.

> *18I speak not of you all: I know whom I have chosen: but that the scripture may be fulfilled: He that eateth my bread lifted up his heel against me. 19From henceforth I tell you before it come to pass, that, when it is come to pass, ye may believe that I am he. 20Verily, verily, I say unto you, he that receiveth whomsoever I send receiveth me; and he that receiveth me receiveth him that sent me.*

John lets us in on what was going on behind the scene. Jesus knows who will betray Him, but He allows history to play out as the Father has ordained it. This is not theatrics. It is obedience. God the Son could have changed the course of history as decreed by the Father, but He chose to obey. The Father's will was His will also.

> *21 When Jesus had thus said, he was troubled in the spirit, and testified, and said, Verily, verily, I say unto you, that one of you shall betray me. 22 The disciples looked one on another, doubting of whom he spake. 23 There was at the table reclining in Jesus' bosom one of his disciples, whom Jesus loved. 24 Simon Peter therefore beckoneth to him, and saith unto him, Tell us who it is of whom he speaketh. 25 He leaning back, as he was, on Jesus' breast saith unto him, Lord, who is it? 26 Jesus therefore answereth, He it is, for whom I shall dip the sop, and give it him.*

Jesus finished His explanation of true servanthood, that it is following His example and being His messenger, then moved to His concern about His betrayer. How much time elapsed between the discussion about servanthood and the discussion of the betrayer? What was the connection? Did the conversation on servanthood lead to thoughts of His final act of servanthood on earth, and did that in turn prompt thoughts about who would initiate that final act? What pain and disappointment Judas' betrayal gave Jesus! The beauty and the purity of the Last Supper was marred by the presence of evil. On earth is it always so? Among the servants Jesus sends out, who go in His Name, are there always traitors?

So when he had dipped the sop, he taketh and giveth it to Judas, the son of Simon Iscariot. 27And after the sop, then entered Satan into him. Jesus therefore saith unto him, What thou doest, do quickly. 28Now no man at the table knew for what intent he spake this unto him. 29For some thought, because Judas had the bag, that Jesus said unto him, Buy what things we have need of for the feast; or, that he should give something to the poor. 30He then having received the sop went out straightway: and it was night.

Why did none of the disciples ask Jesus openly who the betrayer was? They all wanted to know, and Jesus told the one person who asked. Were they all that confused and afraid of Jesus, that they could not be direct with Him? How many opportunities do we lose by not asking God directly what's going on?

That Satan entered into Judas after Jesus gave Judas the bread reflects that Jesus had the power to stay Satan's action until the right moment. Scripture says Judas had already decided to betray Jesus. This, verse 27, just describes the moment Judas was inspired to act on his decision.

31When therefore he was gone out, Jesus saith, Now is the Son of man glorified, and God is glorified in him; 32and God shall glorify him in himself, and straightway shall he glorify him.

Jesus was alone in His understanding of the moment. His companions were clueless. In their ignorance, they could not comfort Him. But He had the Father's assurance.

33Little children, yet a little while I am with you. Ye shall seek me: and as I said unto the Jews, Whither I go, ye cannot come;

The disciples cannot go now, but they will go later. The "Jews" of whom Jesus spoke would never go. Never go? Or might some of their hearts still be transformed?

> *so now I say unto you. 34A new commandment I give unto you, that ye love one another; even as I have loved you, that ye also love one another. 35By this shall all men know that ye are my disciples, if ye have love one to another.*

When Jesus leaves them, what will hold them together? Love. Without love there would be no church.

> *36Simon Peter saith unto him, Lord, whither goest thou? Jesus answered, Whither I go, thou canst not follow now; but thou shalt follow afterwards. 37Peter saith unto him, Lord, why cannot I follow thee even now? I will lay down my life for thee. 38Jesus answereth, Wilt thou lay down thy life for me? Verily, verily, I say unto thee, The cock shall not crow, till thou hast denied me thrice.*

Jesus was ready to enter into glory but He didn't want to leave His disciples alone. They could not join Him in Heaven yet and He was sad to leave them behind. He knew – they did not – how they would suffer because they were His. "You can't go with Me now, but you will follow Me later." "Why can't I go with You now Lord?" "I am ready to die for You." (NLT.) Peter had a confused understanding of what was going on and he was not ready, nor was it the time, for him to go with Jesus into death. But he would go later.

Chapter 14: Believe in Me: I Am the way; ask anything in My name.

> *John 14 (ASV) 1Let not your heart be troubled: believe in God, believe also in me.*

John 14:1 is my salvation verse. But when I heard it, it meant something different to me than it meant to the disciples when they heard it at the Last Supper. Nonetheless, what Jesus said to me in this verse is true and was His message for me individually. That is how the Spirit works. When I heard Him I was asking the question, "God, are You real? Is Jesus Your Son?" Jesus personally answered the question. "Believe in God. Believe also in Me." (ASV) At that point in my life, Heaven was just icing on the cake. I wanted to know the truth: was God real? Was Jesus His Son? If so, I was prepared to give my life to Him, because He is true.

> *2In my Father's house are many mansions; if it were not so, I would have told you; for I go to prepare a place for you. 3And if I go and prepare a place for you, I come again, and will receive you unto myself; that where I am, there ye may be also. 4And whither I go, ye know the way.*

They had just finished a discussion on Jesus' death and Peter's imminent betrayal, when Jesus said, "Let not your hearts be troubled." How could they not be troubled? He

points them to a glorious future. He is going to Heaven
to prepare a place for them, and then He will come get
them. What does He have to do "to prepare a place"? Does
it include more than His death, resurrection, and ascension? What more? Surely something since He still hasn't
come back. Or has He? "When everything is ready" He
will come. What has to happen for everything to be ready?
Heaven won't be ready until the last soul destined for the
Kingdom is ushered in. What else? History has to complete its course, whatever that is. Lord, when I die, is that
when "everything is ready" (NLT) for me and You come to
get me, so I can always be with You? Is this promise both
for the end time and for the individual? You were speaking to individuals who probably regarded the two events
as one, but that's not necessarily how You meant it. Lord,
what are You doing to prepare a place for me? And what
has to happen for it to be ready for me – so many individuals have come to You before the end time. Is Your work
in Heaven really preparing me for Heaven? You are in-
terceding for me, working through the Holy Spirit in and
around me. And then You tell me I know the way to where
You are going. I guess that means that I am to get started
on the way, while I wait for You to finish preparations for
me. The pilgrim's progress.

Heaven wasn't ready for the human race until Jesus died
and rose and ascended – He has prepared the way for us.
And we travel toward it individually. At the right time He
will take each of us to it, to be with Him. And at the right
time He will come to Earth and collect His church and
deliver her to Heaven.

5Thomas saith unto him, Lord, we know not whither thou goest; how know we the way? 6Jesus saith unto him, I am the way, and the truth, and the life: no one cometh unto the Father, but by me. 7If ye had known me, ye would have known my Father also: from henceforth ye know him, and have seen him.

Thomas didn't think he knew the way, because He was thinking in a material time and space sort of way, as I would have. Jesus was going somewhere – somewhere is a material concept, a locatable place in space. Jesus said He was "the way, and the truth, and the life." He thus oriented Thomas to how to find the place to which He is going. It must have been discouraging to Thomas to hear, "If you had really known me" (NLT), as certainly Thomas thought, after three years, he did know Jesus. But then came the assurance, "from now on you do know Him (the Father)." (NLT.) Jesus was going to the Father. If you had seen Jesus, you had seen the Father. How do you get to the Father? Thomas knew: trust and obey Jesus.

8Philip saith unto him, Lord, show us the Father, and it sufficeth us.

After Jesus said that anyone who had seen Him had seen the Father, Phillip asked to see the Father. What boldness! Everyone who seeks the truth does want to "see" the Father, I suppose. Phillip could not comprehend that in knowing Jesus, he did know the Father.

9Jesus saith unto him, Have I been so long time with you, and dost thou not know me, Philip? he that hath seen me hath seen the Father; how sayest thou, Show us the Father? 10Believest thou not that I am in the

*Father, and the Father in me? the words that I say
unto you I speak not from myself: but the Father abiding in me doeth his works. 11Believe me that I am in
the Father, and the Father in me: or else believe me for
the very works' sake.*

Jesus had to break it down into small bites of reality for
Phillip. Believe that the Father is in Jesus, and that Jesus is
in the Father – the Father is both in Him and surrounds
Him. Or, if your heart is too dull to comprehend this incredible spiritual reality, believe Jesus' words for the more
mundane reason that you have seen Him perform miracles by the power the Father vested in Him. This is the
same thing Jesus told the Jews.

*12Verily, verily, I say unto you, he that believeth on
me, the works that I do shall he do also; and greater
works than these shall he do; because I go unto the Father. 13And whatsoever ye shall ask in my name, that
will I do, that the Father may be glorified in the Son.
14If ye shall ask anything in my name, that will I do.*

The incredible words of challenge for the believer: if you
believe in Jesus, He will empower you to do greater works
than He did. When you ask in Jesus' name (according to
His nature), He brings glory to His Father by answering
your prayers In ages past, Christians have asked for the
world, and Jesus gave it to them, for the glory of the Father. Do we still trust Jesus for the world? Do we love Him
enough to ask for the world? Or do we love the world so
much we are satisfied to live in it, rather than to conquer
it for Jesus' sake?

*15If ye love me, ye will keep my commandments.
16And I will pray the Father, and he shall give you*

another Comforter, that he may be with you for ever, 17even the Spirit of truth: whom the world cannot receive; for it beholdeth him not, neither knoweth him: ye know him; for he abideth with you, and shall be in you. 18I will not leave you desolate: I come unto you. 19Yet a little while, and the world beholdeth me no more; but ye behold me: because I live, ye shall live also. 20In that day ye shall know that I am in my Father, and ye in me, and I in you. 21He that hath my commandments, and keepeth them, he it is that loveth me: and he that loveth me shall be loved of my Father, and I will love him, and will manifest myself unto him.

"If you love me, keep my commandments." (NLT.) Lord, you know whether and how much I love You. I know my obedience should come from my love and not be my frantic desire to prove my love. Then You tell me, if I love and obey You, You will ask and the Father will give me the Holy Spirit, who will keep me right. But how can I obey You without the Holy Spirit's help? How can I truly love You without the Holy Spirit? Are You asking me to give what I cannot possible give? Or does "and" not connote sequence, but coincidence? My love, my obedience, Your provision of the Holy Spirit all come at once, together, at the Father's command? You mention my love first because I am aware of it first. And I have the assurance of the Holy Spirit because I know I love.

You tell Your disciples they know the Holy Spirit, because He was with them now and would be in them. Of course, that does not describe me. My experience of You is after Your glorification. My first experience of the Holy Spirit was when He came to dwell in me. (Or was it? Didn't the Holy Spirit testify to me at times before He came to live in me? Upon reflection, yes, He did.) Before Jesus was glorified, the Holy Spirit was with His people, though not dwelling in them. Oh the joy and honor of living on this side of the cross!

"I will come to You." (NLT.) When the Spirit comes, Jesus comes. When Jesus comes, the Father comes. "I am in my Father, you are in me, and I am in you." (NLT.) This is reality in the spiritual universe. I am in Jesus and He is in me. I am accepted by the Father because I am in Jesus. "I will … reveal myself to each of them." (NLT.) You have time for me!

> 22Judas (not Iscariot) saith unto him, Lord, what is come to pass that thou wilt manifest thyself unto us, and not unto the world?

A good question! Judas (not Iscariot) did not expect the peoples of the world to be divided yet again into those who know and belong to God and those who do not. He was expecting the end of the age. Instead, he got the beginning of a new age.

> 23Jesus answered and said unto him, If a man love me, he will keep my word: and my Father will love him, and we will come unto him, and make our abode with him. 24He that loveth me not keepeth not my words: and the word which ye hear is not mine, but the Father's who sent me.
>
> 25These things have I spoken unto you, while yet abiding with you. 26But the Comforter, even the Holy Spirit, whom the Father will send in my name, he

shall teach you all things, and bring to your remem-
brance all that I said unto you.

The other Judas asks, Jesus, why are You leaving the world
in ignorance of You? Jesus doesn't give a straightforward
answer, but isn't He saying that His way of revealing Himself to the world is going to be through those whom He
leaves behind as witnesses? The world will see God in us,
and people will either come to Him or reject Him, based
on our witness and the work of the Holy Spirit.

> *27Peace I leave with you; my peace I give unto you:*
> *not as the world giveth, give I unto you. Let not your*
> *heart be troubled, neither let it be fearful. 28Ye heard*
> *how I said to you, I go away, and I come unto you. If*
> *ye loved me, ye would have rejoiced, because I go unto*
> *the Father: for the Father is greater than I.*

Rejoice for Jesus! He is going home, where He belongs!

> *29And now I have told you before it come to pass,*
> *that, when it is come to pass, ye may believe.*

Lord, unlike those who were with You in the upper room,
it is easy for me to be happy that You left them and went
to Heaven. I gained You because of it. I have the joy of
seeing You glorified, and of being a recipient of Your salvation, which I would never have had it You had not "left."

> *30I will no more speak much with you, for the prince of*
> *the world cometh: and he hath nothing in me; 31but*
> *that the world may know that I love the Father, and*
> *as the Father gave me commandment, even so I do.*
> *Arise, let us go hence.*

Jesus calls Satan the ruler of "this world" – the material
God-denying world. But the "ruler of this world" does not

rule Jesus, because Jesus obeys the Father and the Father uses "the ruler of this world" for His own purposes. Like every created thing, Satan has a role to play in God's master plan.

Chapter 15: The first fruit, so to speak, of living in the Vine is fellowship with Christ. The fruit of such fellowship is obedience. The fruit of obedience is love. The fruits of love are disciples.

> *John 15 (ASV) 1I am the true vine, and my Father is the husbandman. 2Every branch in me that beareth not fruit, he taketh it away: and every branch that beareth fruit, he cleanseth it, that it may bear more fruit. 3Already ye are clean because of the word which I have spoken unto you. 4Abide in me, and I in you. As the branch cannot bear fruit of itself, except it abide in the vine; so neither can ye, except ye abide in me.*

"You have already been pruned and purified by the message I have given you." (NLT.) How does Your message prune and purify me, Lord? When You spoke to your disciples, You were speaking to men whose lives had been transformed by living with You for three years. Your message had seeped into every corner of their lives. What was useless for their discipleship they had already cast away. What sin they had was cleansed daily by confrontation with You and repentance. I am not on the highways of Galilee, Lord, but can my life be like that – pruned and purified on a continuous basis? Cause me, help me, to remain in You.

> *5I am the vine, ye are the branches: He that abideth in me, and I in him, the same beareth much fruit: for*

apart from me ye can do nothing. 6If a man abide not in me, he is cast forth as a branch, and is withered; and they gather them, and cast them into the fire, and they are burned.

"...apart from Me you can do nothing." "When you produce much fruit, you are My true disciples." (NLT.) That's what I want to focus on, Lord, but I fret about those branches that wither, are cast away, and burned. Am I afraid of being one, or of knowing many such branches? "I am the vine, you are the branches." What is pruned, our dead works, will be burned, without destroying our immortal souls. But the branch cut off from the Vine in its entirety is gone! That is Israel. Who else is it? Jesus described the branches that are burned as branches that "abide not in me." Such a branch was not part of the vine. It was already dead before it was burned.

7If ye abide in me, and my words abide in you, ask whatsoever ye will, and it shall be done unto you. 8Herein is my Father glorified, that ye bear much fruit; and so shall ye be my disciples.

What did Jesus mean by a fruitful life? I tend automatically to think of the fruit of the Spirit, but surely He meant producing other disciples. I don't measure up so well on the fruit of the Sprit, but I really don't measure up on the fruit of disciple-making! (Who are my fruit? Name them. Most I am naming are recent. What about my early years as a Christian? I challenged a lot more people, but I don't remember much fruit from back then. Lord, please give me opportunities and grace to produce fruit!)

You cannot produce fruit unless you abide! Jesus' first instruction is to abide in Him. Then the fruit will come. A Christian must first abide in Christ. This is a full-time occupation. A Christian must also produce fruit, but only the Christian who abides in Christ can produce fruit. There is no point laboring to produce fruit if you aren't abiding in Christ. It all happens on the Father's timetable. Abiding and bearing fruit happen together, but it starts with abiding. "[A]bide in My love." (ASV)

Even when you are in the Vine, strong and healthy and growing, it is God who produces the fruit. Never rely on yourself!

> *9Even as the Father hath loved me, I also have loved you:*

What a statement! Christ loves me in the same way the Father loves Him! How can that be? But how is the Father's love for the Son different from the Son's love for the Father? Is there that same difference between the Son's love for me and my love for Him? Is there a difference in the quality of the love, or only in the way the love is demonstrated? In the Son, the quality is the same and the way it is demonstrated is different. In us, the quality if immeasurably inferior, but it can still be real, and pleasing to God the Son (and His Father).

> *abide ye in my love.*

Just as Jesus abides in His Father's love, I am to abide in Jesus' love! Christ's love and the work of His love has raised beings made out of dirt to share in the divine love!

> *10If ye keep my commandments, ye shall abide in my love; even as I have kept my Father's commandments, and abide in his love. 11These things have I spoken*

unto you, that my joy may be in you, and that your joy may be made full.

As much as Jesus loves me His joy will not be "full" because of me. But my joy can be full because of Him.

12This is my commandment, that ye love one another, even as I have loved you. 13Greater love hath no man than this, that a man lay down his life for his friends.

I can love others with the same self-sacrificing love with which Jesus loves me.

14Ye are my friends, if ye do the things which I command you. 15No longer do I call you servants; for the servant knoweth not what his lord doeth: but I have called you friends; for all things that I heard from my Father, I have made known unto you.

The new commandment: "Love each other." (NLT.) Jesus says He loved His disciples just as the Father loved Him. They are His children. They are His friends. "There is no greater love than to lay down your life for your friends." ... "You are my friends, if you do what I command you." "Love each other." "Remain in My love." (NLT.) – by obeying My commandment to love each other.

16Ye did not choose me, but I chose you, and appointed you, that ye should go and bear fruit, and that your fruit should abide: that whatsoever ye shall ask of the Father in my name, he may give it you. 17These things I command you, that ye may love one another.

Lord, is this for me, or just for those disciples? When You said it, You knew them well and had a firm relationship with them. I wasn't born yet. Now that I am, I am developing a relationship with You 2000 years after You said this. Truly, do I have such a relationship with You that I am Your child and Your friend? If I have received Your word, if I abide in You, if I obey Your commandment, then, yes.

The disciples were Jesus' friends and He laid down His life for them. Jesus laid down His life for me. He befriended me. The disciples were His friends because they did what He commanded and He shared with them what the Father had told Him – you confide in your friends. That is a hallmark of friendship. Jesus chooses His friends. He appoints them a job to do and the Father empowers them to do it. Jesus is not a friend among equals. He is both Lord and friend. To be a friend of Jesus is an indescribable honor; it requires obedience, submission to His commandments and will. His commandment is to love. His will is to produce fruit. Does Jesus confide in me? Do I love? Am I producing fruit? Am I a friend to Jesus?

18If the world hateth you, ye know that it hath hated me before it hated you. 19If ye were of the world, the world would love its own: but because ye are not of the world, but I chose you out of the world, therefore the world hateth you. 20Remember the word that I said unto you, A servant is not greater than his lord. If they persecuted me, they will also persecute you; if they kept my word, they will keep yours also. 21But all these things will they do unto you for my name's sake, because they know not him that sent me. 22If I had not come and spoken unto them, they had not had sin: but now they have no excuse for their sin. 23He that hateth me hateth my Father also. 24If I had not done

among them the works which none other did, they had
not had sin: but now have they both seen and hated
both me and my Father. 25But this cometh to pass,
that the word may be fulfilled that is written in their
law, They hated me without a cause.

It seems to me this passage is written particularly in regard to these eleven disciples and that particular time. The
"world" Jesus particularly had in mind that hated Him and
would hate His disciples was the Jewish leaders' world –
those who personally heard Him and personally saw His
miracles. Their hatred of Him and His followers was based
on their knowledge of Him. Later groups would persecute
Jesus' followers in ignorance – and many would eventually be saved. Jesus' special condemnation is for those who
persecute Him and His followers because they do know
who He is. Of course, Satan is "the ruler of this world,"
and He persecutes Jesus' followers for the same reason the
Jewish leaders did – he hates God.

26But when the Comforter is come, whom I will send
unto you from the Father, even the Spirit of truth,
which proceedeth from the Father, he shall bear wit-
ness of me: 27and ye also bear witness, because ye
have been with me from the beginning.

Jesus promises the Holy Spirit will be with the His followers. He will testify to the followers and the followers will
testify about Jesus. Those original eleven would also testify about their original earthly experiences with Jesus. To
them He entrusted the production of the written record
of His life and work an Earth – the explanation of the gospel, the mystery of the ages. Much as I want to claim ev-

erything the apostles had for myself, I cannot. Those who lived with Jesus while He was on earth in human form had and will always have a special relationship with Him and a special place in His heart. How could they not? With them He learned what it was to be human.

Chapter 16: Jesus tells His disciples beforehand so that they will understand later: the Holy Spirit is coming; when you are alone in the world, you are not alone.

> *John 16 (ASV) 1These things have I spoken unto you, that ye should not be caused to stumble. 2They shall put you out of the synagogues: yea, the hour cometh, that whosoever killeth you shall think that he offereth service unto God. 3And these things will they do, because they have not known the Father, nor me. 4But these things have I spoken unto you, that when their hour is come, ye may remember them, how that I told you. And these things I said not unto you from the beginning, because I was with you.*

The fact that Jesus told His disciples in advance what they would suffer helped them when the suffering came, because they understood it was part of His plan. Suffering was not a sign of His defeat, but of His ultimate victory. Are there things Jesus has told me in advance? Yes, perhaps these same things.

> *5But now I go unto him that sent me; and none of you asketh me, Whither goest thou?*

Yet in John 14:8 Thomas said he did not know where Jesus was going. Did he really need to ask specifically? Or was Jesus pointing out to His disciples that they were so consumed by their immediate circumstances that they were not focusing on the bigger picture – where Jesus was going and what that meant for their souls?

> *6But because I have spoken these things unto you, sorrow hath filled your heart. 7Nevertheless I tell you the truth: It is expedient for you that I go away; for if I go not away, the Comforter will not come unto you; but if I go, I will send him unto you.*

The reason the Holy Spirit could not come (that is, dwell in us) before Jesus returned to Heaven is that the requirements of our justification had to be fulfilled in history before God could dwell in us. We are now pure and free from sin in God's eyes, because we are clothed in Christ's righteousness – this clothing is not an idea or a metaphor, it is a reality that makes God's present indwelling possible. God inhabits eternity, but we inhabit the here and now. The Holy Spirit came to dwell in us when history caught up with God's plan for the ages.

> *8And he, when he is come, will convict the world in respect of sin, and of righteousness, and of judgment: 9of sin, because they believe not on me; 10of righteousness, because I go to the Father, and ye behold me no more; 11of judgment, because the prince of this world hath been judged. 12I have yet many things to say unto you, but ye cannot bear them now.*

The reason the Holy Spirit convicts the world of sin, and of God's righteousness, and of the coming judgment is this: when Christ took on our sin and punishment, and was raised to life again, and ascended to sit at the Father's right hand He activated and demonstrated those three principles. The sin of the world is now irrefutably obvious – it has rejected its Savior. God's righteousness is now beyond human dispute, as it is demonstrated in Christ's substitutionary death and resurrection. Likewise, the judgment has now been demonstrated in Christ's death and resurrection, He has triumphed over the powers of evil at work in the world – evil has been conclusively judged and will be defeated.

> 13Howbeit when he, the Spirit of truth, is come, he shall guide you into all the truth: for he shall not speak from himself; but what things soever he shall hear, these shall he speak: and he shall declare unto you the things that are to come. 14He shall glorify me: for he shall take of mine, and shall declare it unto you. 15All things whatsoever the Father hath are mine: therefore said I, that he taketh of mine, and shall declare it unto you.

"When the Spirit of truth comes, He will guide you into all truth." ... "The Spirit will tell you whatever It receives from Me." (NLT.) Lord, was this for the eleven or for all believers? I know that you sent the Holy Spirit to indwell all believers. But how much truth did the Spirit impart to the eleven that He does not impart to believers since then? Only the writing of the New Testament scriptures? Lord, are You guiding me into all truth? Are You having the Spirit tell me whatever it receives from You? I have the written Word and You speak to me through it, as the Spirit applies it to my heart. Do these verses also assure me of Your guidance in my daily life? For the eleven this wasn't an issue, but for everyone since then, it is. We do not want to presume You are going to guide us in a way that is closed to us; but we also do not want to neglect an opportunity for fellowship and communication with You that You are offering us. Perhaps the way we find out what You are offering us is to live in it and experience it, to the extent You offer it – that is a lively and active faith, isn't it?

> *16A little while, and ye behold me no more; and again a little while, and ye shall see me. 17Some of his disciples therefore said one to another, What is this that he saith unto us, A little while, and ye behold me not; and again a little while, and ye shall see me: and, Because I go to the Father? 18They said therefore, What is this that he saith, A little while? We know not what he saith. 19Jesus perceived that they were desirous to ask him, and he said unto them, Do ye inquire among yourselves concerning this, that I said, A little while, and ye behold me not, and again a little while, and ye shall see me? 20Verily, verily, I say unto you, that ye shall weep and lament, but the world shall rejoice: ye shall be sorrowful, but your sorrow shall be turned into joy.*

Jesus spoke in a riddle about His death, instead of just telling them. "In a little while you won't see me anymore. Then …." (NLT.) The riddle was His mechanism for controlling their reactions and their behavior at the point of His arrest. He needed to tell them many things, but if it had been in the context of, "I'm going to die now," they would have been too upset to listen. They might have taken over the conversation with desperate questions, "Why don't we…."

> *21A woman when she is in travail hath sorrow, because her hour is come: but when she is delivered of*

the child, she remembereth no more the anguish, for the joy that a man is born into the world.

Jesus uses childbirth as a comparison for the joy the disciples will feel upon Jesus' resurrection. Has childbirth always, throughout history and culture, been such a joyous occasion? Not just a transient phase in a young couple's life, but a common marker of the character of humanity?

22And ye therefore now have sorrow: but I will see you again, and your heart shall rejoice, and your joy no one taketh away from you.

"[Y]ou will rejoice, and no one can rob you of that joy." (NLT.) The resurrection is the joy of every Christian. It stands forever as the marker of God's love, power, and reality in the affairs of men.

23And in that day ye shall ask me no question. Verily, verily, I say unto you, if ye shall ask anything of the Father, he will give it you in my name. 24Hitherto have ye asked nothing in my name: ask, and ye shall receive, that your joy may be made full.

From henceforth, Christians will pray in Jesus' name. The faithful had not done this before. Now they will. Jesus tells His disciples that after His resurrection, they won't come to Him with their questions and requests. They will go to the Father directly, but they will ask the Father in Jesus' name. Why? Because after the resurrection, the world of men will be operating under a different spiritual regime. People can now experience salvation in real time; they experience God the Father, Son, and Holy Spirit enter their minds and hearts and dwell with them in close communion. This can happen only through Jesus and what He accomplished in His death and resurrection. The believer is safe and blessed in Jesus. The Father blesses the believer in Jesus. The only place the believer is safe and blessed by the Father is in Jesus. To come to the Father outside of Jesus is presumption, worse than useless. (But to the one outside of Jesus who is truly seeking the Father, Jesus offers Himself.)

> *25These things have I spoken unto you in dark sayings: the hour cometh, when I shall no more speak unto you in dark sayings, but shall tell you plainly of the Father.*

Jesus assures the disciples that after the resurrection He will speak plainly and explain things clearly. And He did.

> *26In that day ye shall ask in my name: and I say not unto you, that I will pray the Father for you; 27for the Father himself loveth you, because ye have loved me, and have believed that I came forth from the Father.*

When a Christian asks in Jesus' name, the Father hears and answers. The Father loves the Christian, who loves the Son. Jesus does intercede for us, but the Father hears us directly and responds to us, because we are right there, in His Son.

> *28I came out from the Father, and am come into the world: again, I leave the world, and go unto the Father.*

In answer to one of the questions that so plagued the Jews of Jesus' time, Jesus explained He came from the Father in Heaven to the world, and would return to the person and place, the Father in Heaven, from whence He came.

Before He was born, He was, and after He died, He was, with the Father.

> *29His disciples say, Lo, now speakest thou plainly, and speakest no dark saying. 30Now know we that thou knowest all things, and needest not that any man should ask thee: by this we believe that thou camest forth from God. 31Jesus answered them, Do ye now believe? 32Behold, the hour cometh, yea, is come, that ye shall be scattered, every man to his own, and shall leave me alone: and yet I am not alone, because the Father is with me.*

How pathetic. Really. The disciples claimed they now understood and believed Jesus came from God and was going back to God. What did they think they understood? How firm was their conviction? Jesus knew.

> *33These things have I spoken unto you, that in me ye may have peace. In the world ye have tribulation: but be of good cheer; I have overcome the world.*

Jesus assured them, in spite of their faithlessness, He would be OK. They could have peace knowing He did not die alone. He also forewarned them of their fate – trials and sorrow in the world, but joy in Christ, who overcame the world.

Chapter 17: Jesus talks to His Father about: the Father's Glory; the Glory that is Jesus'; the Glory that He gives to His disciples.

John 17 (ASV) 1These things spake Jesus; and lifting up his eyes to heaven, he said, Father, the hour is come; glorify thy Son, that the Son may glorify thee: 2even as thou gavest him authority over all flesh, that to all whom thou hast given him, he should give eternal life. 3And this is life eternal, that they should know thee the only true God, and him whom thou didst send, even Jesus Christ. 4I glorified thee on the earth, having accomplished the work which thou hast given me to do. 5And now, Father, glorify thou me with thine own self with the glory which I had with thee before the world was.

Jesus speaks to the Father. He is entering the crisis of His life, in utter dependence on the Father, to glorify the Father. He asks, "Glorify Your Son." What does that signify? It means, "Now Father, bring Me into the glory We shared before the world began." (NLT.) When Jesus turned Himself over to men and to Satan to do their best to destroy Him, He gave up His own power as the Second Person of the Trinity and trusted utterly to the Father to rescue Him from death and bring Him back to Heaven. Jesus had authority in Himself, but He gave it up in order to glorify the Father and save men. He glorified the Father by giving up His authority, by obeying and trusting the Father with His life. Jesus has the authority to save each person, but to do it, He had to suffer, die, rise. "... this is the way to have eternal life, to know You, the only true God, and Jesus Christ, the One You sent to earth." (NLT.) Eternal life is having an intimate relationship with God. Jesus died so that we (I) could enter into that knowledge.

"And now, Father, glorify thou me with thine own self with the glory which I had with thee before the world was." (ASV) Jesus' faith in the Father! He never doubted, but He still asked. He asked so that we would understand.

Verses 1-5 introduce the drama that is about to unfold. The epic battle between God and the forces of sin is about to enter the turning point – the decisive confrontation. The stakes are the souls of men and the glory of God the Father. All rides on Jesus' perseverance in faith.

> *6I manifested thy name unto the men whom thou gavest me out of the world: thine they were, and thou gavest them to me; and they have kept thy word. 7Now they know that all things whatsoever thou hast given me are from thee: 8for the words which thou gavest me I have given unto them; and they received them, and knew of a truth that I came forth from thee, and they believed that thou didst send me.*

Why did Jesus prove who He was in the manner in which He did? If God was going to become man, why would He choose to manifest Himself in the life and death Jesus experienced? To outsiders that is a crucial question about the Gospel. The disciples belonged to the Father. The Father gave them to the Son. The Son "passed on to them the message [the Father] gave [the Son]." The disciples "accepted it and know that I came from You, and they believe[d] You sent me." (NLT.) If convincing them He was the Son of God was such a critical part of His mission, why did He do it the way He did? As Jesus Himself said, if you are looking for a king, you go to a palace. Jesus came as He did because He wasn't interested in raw power – He had that before He came to earth – He was interested in transformative power, the power to change hearts and minds, to provoke willing worship and surrender of all of one's being. The source of transformative power is love, not fear. Jesus proved who He was by loving His disciples as only God could love them. His miracles were tangible proofs of His love. He healed, He fed, He forgave, He reconciled man to God. He sought true worshipers, not rats deserting a sinking ship.

> 9I pray for them: I pray not for the world, but for those whom thou hast given me; for they are thine: 10and all things that are mine are thine, and thine are mine: and I am glorified in them. 11And I am no more in the world, and these are in the world, and I come to thee. Holy Father, keep them in thy name which thou hast given me, that they may be one, even as we are. 12While I was with them, I kept them in thy name which thou hast given me: and I guarded them, and not one of them perished, but the son of perdition; that the scripture might be fulfilled.

The Church Age is a difficult time, but God protects His own. We are "in the world," because we have an assignment to complete. We are safe from Satan's power – we cannot be overcome by Satan – Jesus asks the Father to "protect them [us] by the power of Your name so that they will be united just as We are." (NLT.) The Father gave Jesus His power [power in the Father's name] while Jesus was on earth. While Jesus was on earth did He always act in the power of the Father's name, when He could have acted in the power of His own [the Son's] name? It seems so. As a man, Jesus always relied on the Father and the Father's power. Though God, Jesus never relied on His own power. While a man, He was united to the Father in a different way than He had been in Heaven. On earth, Jesus' submission to His Father was absolute. He proved, that is, lived out His love by perfect obedience and trust. If any ever born could have relied on his own strength, it was Jesus, but He didn't.

> *13But now I come to thee; and these things I speak in the world, that they may have my joy made full in themselves. 14I have given them thy word; and the world hated them, because they are not of the world, even as I am not of the world. 15I pray not that thou shouldest take them from the world, but that thou shouldest keep them from the evil one. 16They are not of the world even as I am not of the world. 17Sanctify them in the truth: thy word is truth. 18As thou didst send me into the world, even so sent I them into the world. 19And for their sakes I sanctify myself, that they themselves also may be sanctified in truth.*

What do you want for Your disciples, Lord? That we …. remember what You told us; that we would be filled with Your joy; that we keep the Father's word in our hearts. You asked the Father to keep us safe from the evil one. We do not belong to this world, but You keep us here for a reason. You asked the Father to teach us Your word, to make us holy. You sacrificed Yourself to make us holy, and You have sent us into the world to save the world. That's why we're here. While You were here on earth, You taught and trained Your disciples and brought sinners into Your kingdom. You are leaving me here to do the same. But what I am offering the world I can only offer if I have it myself. Lord, on this earth I spend more time struggling to follow You, develop Your character, fellowship with You, worship You properly, than I do reaching out to the world. You didn't have to spend all that time on Yourself when You were here. I am both a disciple and a discipler. You were a discipler. You were God most perfect! No wonder my work is so wanting! Lord, Have mercy on me and grow my heart and my ministry by Your power!

> *20Neither for these only do I pray, but for them also that believe on me through their word; 21that they may all be one; even as thou, Father, art in me, and I in thee, that they also may be in us: that the world may believe that thou didst send me.*

I am part of an unbroken line of believers since the Lord and His apostles preached. No generation has failed to produce a cadre of believers who passed on the faith. It would be interesting to trace the line of human instruments from Jesus to me, or any particular believer. Even though I was alone and on my own in thought when the Lord brought me to faith in Him, there were several I knew who testified and prayed for me. Two young women in particular stand out as having taken me on as a project. And what is my role in this, my generation? "And may they be in us so that the world will believe You sent me." (NLT.) I am to have such honest and real fellowship with You and other believers that the world will see it and believe in You, and join me in fellowship with You. So my striving as a disciple is actually part of my testimony!

> *22And the glory which thou hast given me I have given unto them; that they may be one, even as we are one; 23I in them, and thou in me, that they may be perfected into one; that the world may know that thou didst send me, and lovedst them, even as thou lovedst me. 24Father, I desire that they also whom thou hast given me be with me where I am, that they may behold my glory, which thou hast given me: for thou lovedst me before the foundation of the world. 25O righteous Father, the world knew thee not, but I knew thee; and these knew that thou didst send me; 26and I made known unto them thy name, and will make it known; that the love wherewith thou lovedst me may be in them, and I in them.*

"… You love them as much as You love me!" (NLT.) Holy Father, how can that be? I am utterly unlike Jesus and utterly unworthy in comparison to Him. He deserves Your love. "Father, I want these whom You have given Me to be with Me where I am." (NLT.) Thank You, thank You, Lord for wanting me to be with You! You want Your friends and loved ones with You, and You have chosen me as Your friend and loved one. I do not deserve it, I am not suited for it, but I will strive to become suited for it, and You will accomplish the transformation in me. Father, You loved me before I was born, but there is no way I could make myself acceptable to be in Your presence. Jesus loved You so much that He sacrificed His very nature as God and became human flesh in order to do what needed to be done to make me acceptable. If you could love Him more for what He did, You would. Oh that I should love Him fully. Such love honors both the Son and the Father who sent Him.

Chapter 18: Who is on trial?

John 18 (ASV) 1When Jesus had spoken these words, he went forth with his disciples over the brook Kidron, where was a garden, into which he entered, himself and his disciples. 2Now Judas also, who betrayed him, knew the place: for Jesus oft-times resorted thither with his disciples.

There is so much about Jesus' life that we do not know!

3Judas then, having received the band of soldiers, and officers from the chief priests and the Pharisees, cometh thither with lanterns and torches and weapons. 4Jesus therefore, knowing all the things that were coming upon him, went forth, and saith unto them, Whom seek ye?

Let there be no question of who was in control of the situation.

5They answered him, Jesus of Nazareth. Jesus saith unto them, I am he. And Judas also, who betrayed him, was standing with them.

Judas was such a bit player in the story, you have to wonder why God gave him a role at all. What am I supposed to learn from Judas? Even if you are largely ineffectual in your life, the stand you take on Jesus matters to God. Was it important that there was a human betrayer and not just the power of Satan at work in Jesus' arrest? Yes, I am not in control, but I am still responsible

6When therefore he said unto them, I am he, they went backward, and fell to the ground. 7Again therefore he asked them, Whom seek ye? And they said, Jesus of Nazareth. 8Jesus answered, I told you that I am he; if therefore ye seek me, let these go their way: 9that the word might be fulfilled which he spake, Of those whom thou hast given me I lost not one.

Is there anyone else in Scripture or world history before this time who is famous specifically for his self-sacrifice? When Samson brought the temple down, was he thinking about saving his people, or getting revenge? The Spartans died to save Greece from Persian domination, but does history remember them for their self-sacrifice or for their bravery? Only Jesus' self-sacrifice was pure, with no mixed emotions.

10Simon Peter therefore having a sword drew it, and struck the high priest's servant, and cut off his right ear. Now the servant's name was Malchus. 11Jesus therefore said unto Peter, Put up the sword into the sheath: the cup which the Father hath given me, shall I not drink it?

Only John records that it was Peter who cut off Malchus' ear. The Gospel of John does not record Jesus' prayer in the garden or the disciples' falling asleep. How odd; since John would know the importance of that incident better than anyone. Could it be the experience was still too raw and John's concern for Jesus' privacy too strong, for him to include it? John does record the fact that Jesus permitted His arrest – those who came for Him were powerless to arrest Him; so He submitted Himself to it. (John knew

Malchus' name. Was that because John had connections with the priestly clan or because Malchus became a believer?) The other gospels do not record how the crowd fell back when Jesus said, "I Am He." John's perspective on the scene is different. What remains clear in his memory is different from the other writers'. Of Matthew, Mark, Luke, and John, only John was right beside Jesus when the arrest occurred. He saw things others might not have seen or understood.

Why did the posse fall back when Jesus identified Himself? Was it the power of God overwhelming them? Were some of them reluctant to carry out their orders? Either way, the result was they arrested Jesus on His own direction.

> *12So the band and the chief captain, and the officers of the Jews, seized Jesus and bound him, 13and led him to Annas first; for he was father in law to Caiaphas, who was high priest that year. 14Now Caiaphas was he that gave counsel to the Jews, that it was expedient that one man should die for the people.*
>
> *15And Simon Peter followed Jesus, and so did another disciple. Now that disciple was known unto the high priest, and entered in with Jesus into the court of the high priest; 16but Peter was standing at the door without. So the other disciple, who was known unto the high priest, went out and spake unto her that kept the door, and brought in Peter. 17The maid therefore that kept the door saith unto Peter, Art thou also one of this man's disciples? He saith, I am not.*

They first took Jesus to Annas. (Did Annas and Caiaphas live in the same house? Same neighborhood?) Only Peter and John followed. Peter was allowed in because John had connections. Perhaps Peter's first denial of Jesus had the excuse of assuring Peter was admitted – the woman who admitted him asked him. John was in the place, too, yet he focuses his narrative on Peter. It is Jesus' transaction with Peter that John wants to record. John is a witness, not a participant.

18Now the servants and the officers were standing there, having made a fire of coals; for it was cold; and they were warming themselves: and Peter also was with them, standing and warming himself.

This is the kind of detail John uses that draws us into the story. We are there with Peter, experiencing his terror, as he stands in the midst of his enemies.

19The high priest therefore asked Jesus of his disciples, and of his teaching. 20Jesus answered him, I have spoken openly to the world; I ever taught in synagogues, and in the temple, where all the Jews come together; and in secret spake I nothing. 21Why askest thou me? Ask them that have heard me, what I spake unto them: behold, these know the things which I said. 22And when he had said this, one of the officers standing by struck Jesus with his hand, saying, Answerest thou the high priest so? 23Jesus answered him, If I have spoken evil, bear witness of the evil: but if well, why smitest thou me? 24Annas therefore sent him bound unto Caiaphas the high priest.

Jesus was first questioned by Annas, the former high priest. He must still have been a significant power behind Caiaphas, since he got first crack at Jesus. He focused on the threat Jesus' teachings posed. The first assault on Jesus occurred then, when Jesus contested the process and argued with Annas rather than confessing the information Annas wanted. Annas wanted to know who Jesus' followers were and what Jesus taught them. Perhaps he thought Jesus taught a different, more revolutionary, message to His followers than he taught the crowds. Annas knew what Jesus preached in public and that was nothing that should have condemned Him. Annas wanted words he could take out of context and use as justification to condemn Jesus. "If I said anything wrong, you must prove it." (NLT.) Jesus and Annas both knew that the law would not condemn Jesus. In an honest court, Annas' prosecution would have failed. Thus the resort to violence and the power of position. This seems more of a prosecutorial interrogation that a trial. Could we liken it to a preliminary hearing, where the burden on the prosecutor is supposed to be low? When he didn't get an easy answer out of Jesus to justify the arrest, Annas sent Jesus on to Caiaphas – let it be Caiaphas' problem. Jesus is in full control of Himself. Annas had been defeated under the law, but he had an easy out. Evidence doesn't matter. Power does.

> *25Now Simon Peter was standing and warming himself. They said therefore unto him, Art thou also one of his disciples? He denied, and said, I am not. 26One of the servants of the high priest, being a kinsman of him whose ear Peter cut off, saith, Did not I see thee in the garden with him? 27Peter therefore denied again: and straightway the cock crew.*

Peter's second and third denials. He was surrounded by Jesus' enemies. If he were to admit his association with

Jesus, Peter believed he would be handing himself over to the mercy of those who had no mercy. When Peter told Jesus he would never deny Him, this wasn't the circumstance he had envisioned. But isn't that when we are most tested in our faith and love – in the unexpected circumstances in which we feel weakest and most vulnerable? Even when we are exalted, the attack of Satan comes with a challenge that threatens humiliating us, one that would show us undeserving of the attention we are receiving.

> *28They lead Jesus therefore from Caiaphas into the Praetorium:*

John does not describe the trial before Caiaphas. He goes straight to Pilate.

> *and it was early; and they themselves entered not into the Praetorium, that they might not be defiled, but might eat the passover.*

Clearly John is saying that the Last Supper was not the Jewish Passover meal.

> *29Pilate therefore went out unto them, and saith, What accusation bring ye against this man?*

It's surprising Pilate agreed to come out to meet with the Jews. He knew they believed he defiled them, and he probably hated them for it. Perhaps he cared so little for their opinion that making this concession didn't bother him.

> *30They answered and said unto him, If this man were not an evildoer, we should not have delivered him up unto thee. 31Pilate therefore said unto them, Take him yourselves, and judge him according to your law. The Jews said unto him, It is not lawful for us to put*

any man to death: 32that the word of Jesus might be fulfilled, which he spake, signifying by what manner of death he should die.

While the Jews and Pilate parried for control of the situation as they perceived it, God used their pathetic power struggle to advance His Kingdom. The Jews wanted Jesus' execution to be "lawful," which meant crucifixion. Stoning, the Jewish mode of execution, could have given Jesus' followers standing in Roman eyes, in the conflict the Jews imagined might follow.

33Pilate therefore entered again into the Praetorium, and called Jesus, and said unto him, Art thou the King of the Jews?

Pilate didn't worry about defiling Jesus. Nor did the Jews worry about Jesus being defiled by entering Pilate's headquarters. Pilate began the trial by asking Jesus to admit or deny the charge, "Are you the king of the Jews?" (NLT.)

34Jesus answered, Sayest thou this of thyself, or did others tell it thee concerning me? 35Pilate answered, Am I a Jew? Thine own nation and the chief priests delivered thee unto me: what hast thou done? 36Jesus answered, My kingdom is not of this world: if my kingdom were of this world, then would my servants fight, that I should not be delivered to the Jews: but now is my kingdom not from hence.

Pilate's question had been procedurally correct. In a court of the law, the defendant should then admit or deny. Instead, Jesus undertook a discussion with Pilate. He took Pilate's question as a real question and not a legal formality. Pilate pointed out how unusual it was for the Jews

to betray one of their own to the Romans, the Jews' enemy. Pilate's next question "Why? What have you done?"
(NLT.) addressed the human reason Jesus was before him
– what did Jesus do to rile the Jews? Jesus then responded
that He was king of the Jews, but His was not an "earthly kingdom." Jesus was not challenging worldly authority
in order to gain worldly power. He did not challenge the
Sanhedrin for their political power, or Caesar for his. He
did not ask His followers to attack worldly authority with
worldly weapons. In fact, Jesus had broken no law. Nonetheless, as Pilate discovers, Jesus was a dangerous man.

> 37Pilate therefore said unto him, Art thou a king
> then? Jesus answered, Thou sayest that I am a king.
> To this end have I been born, and to this end am I
> come into the world, that I should bear witness unto
> the truth. Every one that is of the truth heareth my
> voice. 38Pilate saith unto him, What is truth?

The truth was uncomfortable ground for Pilate.

> And when he had said this, he went out again unto
> the Jews, and saith unto them, I find no crime in him.
> 39But ye have a custom, that I should release unto
> you one at the passover: will ye therefore that I release
> unto you the King of the Jews? 40They cried out there-
> fore again, saying, Not this man, but Barabbas. Now
> Barabbas was a robber.

"So you are a king?" And Jesus told him, He came "into the
world to testify to the truth. All who love the truth recognize what I say is true." (NLT.) On the one hand, Pilate
responded by asserting there is no truth, that truth is val-
ueless in the face of power. On the other hand, Pilate went

out to the people, to see if they recognized truth in Jesus. They did not. They asked for Barabbas (worldly revolt) over Jesus (heavenly truth). Did Pilate have any anticipation the Jews would choose Jesus over Barabbas? If they were doing as they said, protecting the interests of Rome, they would have chosen to release Jesus over Barabbas. At the very least, this ploy of Pilate's resulted in the Jews being forced to admit their true, self-centered and corrupt motives.

Pilate spoke the truth when he said, "He is not guilty of any crime." (NLT.) But he bowed to the will of the crowd, who did not care about the truth or the law. Pilate was being true to his own nature – even when facing and acknowledging the truth he preferred power. To satisfy his conscience, he passed the buck.

"What is truth?" That God rules over all. That God is Judge and that both the Jews' and Pilate's power structures had been judged and found wanting. While not challenging Rome with physical might, the truth Jesus proclaimed threatened to destroy Rome, Jerusalem, and all power structures that are not built on the truth of God's power. He will destroy them by transforming the hearts of men.

Chapter 19: And Jesus died.

John 19 (ASV) 1 Then Pilate therefore took Jesus, and scourged him.

Why, when Pilate knew Jesus was innocent, did he scourge Him? Was he following procedure? Did he think perversely that he was punishing the Jews by making them act unjustly? Was it part of his strategy to get Jesus released?

2And the soldiers platted a crown of thorns, and put it on his head, and arrayed him in a purple garment; 3and they came unto him, and said, Hail, King of the Jews! and they struck him with their hands.

The recounting of the Lord's torture and humiliation before men who did not know that they themselves were condemned to the torments of hell is so very hard to read. Often we are reading it when our hearts/minds/thoughts are otherwise fixed on pleasant things. When we are suddenly confronted with the horror of our Lord's death, we either flee from our comfort to confront the facts of Jesus death, or we trivialize the facts so that we can return to our comfortable thoughts. Is that what Pilate was doing? God can hold joy and sorrow, peace and anger, horror and bliss in His consciousness at the same time; we cannot. Lord, forgive me for the times I turn away from the reality of Your suffering so that I can go on with my day!

4And Pilate went out again, and saith unto them, Behold, I bring him out to you, that ye may know that I find no crime in him. 5Jesus therefore came out, wearing the crown of thorns and the purple garment.

What did Pilate think would happen? Did he possibly hope to raise an ounce of pity from these Jewish rulers?

And Pilate saith unto them, Behold, the man! 6When therefore the chief priests and the officers saw him, they cried out, saying, Crucify him, crucify him! Pilate saith unto them, Take him yourselves, and crucify him: for I find no crime in him. 7The Jews answered him, We have a law, and by that law he ought to die, because he made himself the Son of God. 8When Pilate therefore heard this saying, he was the more afraid; 9and he entered into the Praetorium again, and saith unto Jesus, Whence art thou? But Jesus gave him no answer.

Why did Jesus give Pilate no answer? Because, from Jesus' perspective the train was on the right track. He had no reason to send Pilate in another direction.

10Pilate therefore saith unto him, Speakest thou not unto me? Knowest thou not that I have power to release thee, and have power to crucify thee? 11Jesus answered him, Thou wouldest have no power against me, except it were given thee from above: therefore he that delivered me unto thee hath greater sin. 12Upon this Pilate sought to release him: but the Jews cried out, saying, If thou release this man, thou art not Caesar's friend: every one that maketh himself a king speaketh against Caesar.

Pilate was caught in the trap Jesus had avoided. How do you reconcile the rule of God with the rule of man? Pilate rejected the truth about God, thinking he could find safety in the power structure the world provided. But he had escaped one dilemma only to be confronted with another. He could not escape the reality of God's inexorable will.

> *13When Pilate therefore heard these words, he brought Jesus out, and sat down on the judgment-seat at a place called The Pavement, but in Hebrew, Gabbatha. 14Now it was the Preparation of the passover: it was about the sixth hour.*

Noon on the day before Passover, which began at 6PM.

> *And he saith unto the Jews, Behold, your King! 15They therefore cried out, Away with him, away with him, crucify him! Pilate saith unto them, Shall I crucify your King? The chief priests answered, We have no king but Caesar.*

The Jews also were caught in the trap Jesus avoided when they set it for Him. To reject Jesus, they had to embrace Caesar. Until Jesus, Caesar had been their greatest enemy.

> *16Then therefore he delivered him unto them to be crucified.*

Pilate repeatedly announced Jesus was innocent; yet he allowed the Jews to have their way and kill Him under the authority of Rome. John does not recount Pilate's trying to foist Jesus off on Herod – it didn't work anyway. Pilate forfeited Roman justice to political expediency. Neither the truth, nor justice, were worth more than keeping peace with the Jews that day. To Pilate, Jesus wasn't worth it. "You would have no power over me at all unless it were given to you from above. So the one who handed me over to you has the greater sin." (NLT.) Pilate was just a cog in the Roman civil service. Caiaphas was the one who chose to kill God. We tend to think of Judas as the evil betrayer, because he was Jesus' trusted and beloved friend; but Caiaphas was the man entrusted by God as high priest to represent the people to God. He was God's ordained leader of the people and he chose to murder God in order to preserve his own position and way of life. To abuse C.S. Lewis' metaphor, he chose playing in the dirt of the Earth over an everlasting vacation in Heaven. Pilate fled from reality. Caiaphas defied it.

17They took Jesus therefore: and he went out, bearing the cross for himself, unto the place called The place of a skull, which is called in Hebrew, Golgotha: 18where they crucified him, and with him two others, on either side one, and Jesus in the midst. 19And Pilate wrote a title also, and put it on the cross. And there was written, JESUS OF NAZARETH, THE KING OF THE JEWS. 20This title therefore read many of the Jews, for the place where Jesus was crucified was nigh to the city; and it was written in Hebrew, and in Latin, and in Greek. 21The chief priests of the Jews therefore said to Pilate, Write not, The King of the Jews; but that he said, I am King of the Jews. 22Pilate answered, What I have written I have written.

"Jesus of Nazareth, the King of the Jews." Pilate wrote it to mock the Jews. He probably didn't care that it mocked Jesus as well. While Pilate was undoubtedly amused by his own wit, the tragic humor of the situation was that what Pilate wrote was true. God used Pilate's words to mock both Roman and Jewish worldly authority. Jesus' crucifixion declared God's control over the affairs of men, as well as His love. God's plan did not condemn the world, but saved it.

> *23 The soldiers therefore, when they had crucified Jesus, took his garments and made four parts, to every soldier a part; and also the coat: now the coat was without seam, woven from the top throughout. 24 They said therefore one to another, Let us not rend it, but cast lots for it, whose it shall be: that the scripture might be fulfilled, which saith,*
>
> *They parted my garments among them,*
>
> *And upon my vesture did they cast lots.*

Psalm 22. Proof of God's control! The soldiers' trivialization of Jesus' suffering – playing a game of chance over Jesus' worldly possessions – had been planned by God since before creation.

> *25 These things therefore the soldiers did. But there were standing by the cross of Jesus his mother, and his mother's sister, Mary the wife of Clopas, and Mary Magdalene. 26 When Jesus therefore saw his mother, and the disciple standing by whom he loved, he saith unto his mother, Woman, behold thy son! 27 Then saith he to the disciple, Behold, thy mother! And from that hour the disciple took her unto his own home.*

The four women at the cross, Mary His mother and her sister, Mary the wife of Clopas, and Mary Magdalene. Is Clopas the same person as Cleopas? If so, then she was the other disciple on the road to Emmaus. John doesn't mention that John's own mother was there – see Matt. 27:56. Perhaps because she, as Matthew says, was "watching from a distance." (NLT.) Or, could she have been Mary's sister? John was recounting what he saw, not everything that was happening. Why did Jesus give the care of His mother to John and not to His own brothers? Perhaps because His brothers were to be martyred and John was ordained to live to an old age – he would be able to care for Mary until she died peacefully.

> 28After this Jesus, knowing that all things are now finished, that the scripture might be accomplished, saith, I thirst. 29There was set there a vessel full of vinegar: so they put a sponge full of the vinegar upon hyssop, and brought it to his mouth. 30When Jesus therefore had received the vinegar, he said, It is finished: and he bowed his head, and gave up his spirit.

Jesus waited to die until he had fulfilled the last prophecy concerning His death. He drank the sour wine and knew He could give up His soul to the Father because it was finished. Did He ask for something to drink because He really was thirsty? Of course. In Scripture, temporal/historical fact and prophetic truth coincide (just as temporal/historical fact and allegorical truth coincide). God is in control of both.

> 31The Jews therefore, because it was the Preparation, that the bodies should not remain on the cross upon the sabbath (for the day of that sabbath was a high day), asked of Pilate that their legs might be broken, and that they might be taken away. 32The soldiers therefore came, and brake the legs of the first, and of the other that was crucified with him: 33but when they came to Jesus, and saw that he was dead already,

they brake not his legs: 34howbeit one of the soldiers with a spear pierced his side, and straightway there came out blood and water. 35And he that hath seen hath borne witness, and his witness is true: and he knoweth that he saith true, that ye also may believe. 36For these things came to pass, that the scripture might be fulfilled, A bone of him shall not be broken. 37And again another scripture saith, They shall look on him whom they pierced.

Is there humor in the fact that, even in murdering God, the Jews wanted to keep some rule about not leaving dead bodies out on the Sabbath? Had the Jews not realized that before the end of the day they were going to need to get home for Passover and Jesus probably wouldn't be dead yet? Perhaps they hadn't thought about that in advance, perhaps they only realized it as the day wore on and they watched Jesus' torment and conduct in His dying. Even for the chief priests, Jesus' death took on a "life" of its own. They felt compelled to see Jesus' death through to the end. They sought to control it by getting Pilate to order Jesus' legs be broken, but even in this the priests did not control the situation. Jesus had already died. Scripture cannot be broken.

When John inserted his authentication of the death of Jesus, he was authenticating the entire event, not just the results of the spear piercing Jesus' side. I suppose the fact that water and blood both flowed out may be evidence that Jesus was conclusively dead. The piercing fulfilled another prophecy, as did Jesus' legs not being broken – the entire crucifixion was under God's control. Lord, knowing that You were in control makes it more bearable to read, but not less horrifying. A death that has meaning is more horrifying than a death that has none. And because Your death mattered, every death matters.

> *38And after these things Joseph of Arimathaea, being a disciple of Jesus, but secretly for fear of the Jews, asked of Pilate that he might take away the body of Jesus: and Pilate gave him leave. He came therefore, and took away his body. 39And there came also Nicodemus, he who at the first came to him by night, bringing a mixture of myrrh and aloes, about a hundred pounds. 40So they took the body of Jesus, and bound it in linen cloths with the spices, as the custom of the Jews is to bury.*

Joseph of Arimathea was a secret disciple "because he feared the Jewish leaders." (NLT.) Joseph showed his loyalties by asking for Jesus' body. Had his being a "secret disciple" during Jesus' life been an act of cowardice or of wisdom under the circumstances? Would history be different if Joseph and Nicodemus had stood up against the Jewish council while Jesus was still preaching? This is only a rhetorical question; history has only one course. Joseph and Nicodemus had probably thought they had time to make a public decision – but they lost their opportunities to side with Jesus during His life on earth. What happened to them afterward? They evidently did not become leaders in the local church – but they still might have been part of the church. And they might have had to flee Jerusalem early on in the Jewish leaders' persecution of the church. Thank You, Lord, for having John include the stories of Nicodemus and Joseph of Arimathea in his gospel narrative.

41Now in the place where he was crucified there was a garden; and in the garden a new tomb wherein was never man yet laid. 42There then because of the Jews' Preparation (for the tomb was nigh at hand) they laid Jesus.

They buried Jesus in a hurry, but tenderly, in compliance with their tradition, as best they could. I suppose there was less danger to them from being exposed as followers of Jesus immediately after His death. Why should Caiaphas care about them now? Their hero was dead and His message had no power.

Chapter 20: The Resurrection!

John 20 (ASV) 1Now on the first day of the week cometh Mary Magdalene early, while it was yet dark, unto the tomb, and seeth the stone taken away from the tomb. 2She runneth therefore, and cometh to Simon Peter, and to the other disciple whom Jesus loved, and saith unto them, They have taken away the Lord out of the tomb, and we know not where they have laid him.

When Mary says "we" she signifies she was not alone when she discovered the empty tomb. John records only Mary Magdalene coming to the tomb. That is what he would have known, since she is the one who came to get him and Peter. She had no clue about the resurrection. She believed in her heart that Jesus was dead.

3Peter therefore went forth, and the other disciple, and they went toward the tomb. 4And they ran both together: and the other disciple outran Peter, and came first to the tomb; 5and stooping and looking in, he seeth the linen cloths lying; yet entered he not in. 6Simon Peter therefore also cometh, following him, and entered into the tomb; and he beholdeth the linen cloths lying, 7and the napkin, that was upon his head, not lying with the linen cloths, but rolled up in a place by itself.

This is so clearly a first-hand account!

John and Peter were running to the same place, the tomb, but they weren't running together. Each was fixed on getting to the tomb. Peter went in first – he was again the bold one. The cloth that had covered Jesus' head was "folded up and lying apart." (NLT.) That tells us something about the way Jesus resurrected. He didn't burst the wrappings and cloth with explosive power. His body was transformed, not obliterated. Did He get up, take off the face cloth, and unwrap Himself; or did he resurrect right through them, leaving the wrappings in a jumble because they were empty, and the face cloth lying separate because that was where His head had been – separated from His body by His neck? Or did He pick up the face cloth after He resurrected and fold it Himself and lay it down separately? As a sign that His life in the old body was over. His work in the old flesh was done. Goodbye to it. Peter and John would have known what He meant.

I think Jesus had hung around the tomb for a minute, and personally folded the face cloth, both as goodbye to the old body and as a sign to Peter. I also think when He resurrected, the wrappings just collapsed because they couldn't contain a spiritual body. Spiritual bodies do not take up material space. They have substance, but not material substance.

> 8 Then entered in therefore the other disciple also, who came first to the tomb, and he saw, and believed. 9For as yet they knew not the scripture, that he must rise from the dead. 10So the disciples went away again unto their own home.

They believed. Even though they didn't understand the prophecy of the resurrection, they understood what they saw. Jesus had been raised from the dead. They went home to wait for Him. I wonder where their "own home" in Jerusalem was.

> *11But Mary was standing without at the tomb weeping: so, as she wept, she stooped and looked into the tomb; 12and she beholdeth two angels in white sitting, one at the head, and one at the feet, where the body of Jesus had lain.*

Why had she not gone into the tomb? If she had not seen the angels, would she have gone in?

> *13And they say unto her, Woman, why weepest thou? She saith unto them, Because they have taken away my Lord, and I know not where they have laid him.*

Mary was undoubtedly processing the new evidence provided by the appearance of the angels, but she answered their question out of the thoughts she was experiencing right before she saw them.

What is true mourning like? It must be all consuming. Not the way people mourn in our society, where you are expected to recover your objectivity within hours. You can stay sad, but you must keep your personal grief in perspective.

> *14When she had thus said, she turned herself back, and beholdeth Jesus standing, and knew not that it was Jesus. 15Jesus saith unto her, Woman, why weepest thou? whom seekest thou? She, supposing him to be the gardener, saith unto him, Sir, if thou hast borne him hence, tell me where thou hast laid him, and I will take him away.*

Mary took responsibility. She couldn't have taken Jesus' body from them, but she thought something needed to be done, and she was the only one available to do it.

> *16Jesus saith unto her, Mary. She turneth herself, and saith unto him in Hebrew, Rabboni; which is to say, Teacher.*

Out of reverence for the moment, John leaves Mary's salutation in Hebrew, instead of translating it into Greek.

God cared enough about Mary Magdalene to send two angels to comfort her and to prepare her to see the risen Jesus. Was there any other reason for angels to be there? Were angels so excited about the resurrection that they came to see it, too?

People think it odd that Mary did not recognize Jesus immediately. It was early morning, not yet fully light, and she was distraught and crying. Her thoughts were focused on the tomb. She was expecting to see anyone but Jesus. It is not surprising that she didn't recognize Him until He spoke. Grief clouds your vision.

> *17Jesus saith to her, Touch me not; for I am not yet ascended unto the Father: but go unto my brethren, and say to them, I ascend unto my Father and your Father, and my God and your God. 18Mary Magdalene cometh and telleth the disciples, I have seen the Lord; and that he had said these things unto her.*

Jesus chose Mary Magdalene to be the first human being He spoke to after His resurrection. He must have had a special love for her, like the one He had for John the Apostle. And He had a special, protective, love for the women who came to the tomb. He provided angels for them, to facilitate their understanding of what had happened.

What did Jesus mean, not to touch Him, that He was ascending to His Father? Had He literally just resurrected and wanted to see Mary before He went to Heaven? He came back to earth many times over the next 40 days, before His final ascension. Eight days after the resurrection, He instructed Thomas to touch Him. I think when He told Mary He had to go to His Father, it was because He had yet to ascend for the very first time. He wanted Mary to share His excitement, and to know that God was her Father, just as He was Jesus' Father.

When we think of Easter, we think of the confusion and excitement going on here on Earth. But think about the excitement in Heaven, when Jesus, the Second Person of the Trinity, the First Fruits of the Dead, the Resurrected King, arrived.

> 19When therefore it was evening, on that day, the first day of the week, and when the doors were shut where the disciples were, for fear of the Jews, Jesus came and stood in the midst, and saith unto them, Peace be unto you. 20And when he had said this, he showed unto them his hands and his side. The disciples therefore were glad, when they saw the Lord.

Though they sort of knew that Jesus was alive, that He had unleashed the power that overcomes death, the apostles were still hiding, "for fear of the Jews."

When Jesus saw His disciples that night, it was after He had been to the Father, but He still had the wounds from

His crucifixion. Lord, I thought our resurrection bodies would be perfect. But Yours is still marred. For all eternity, when we look on You, will we be reminded visibly of what You did for us? Are Your wounds part of Your perfection?

> *21Jesus therefore said to them again, Peace be unto you: as the Father hath sent me, even so send I you. 22And when he had said this, he breathed on them, and saith unto them, Receive ye the Holy Spirit: 23whose soever sins ye forgive, they are forgiven unto them; whose soever sins ye retain, they are retained.*

This was huge. "Receive ye the Holy Spirit." Jesus gave those in the room the indwelling Holy Spirit that very night. He created His Church that very night, and He gave it a commission: "If you forgive anyone's sins, they are forgiven. If you do not forgive them, they are not forgiven." (NLT). What does that mean? We know that only God can forgive sins. But God in the form of the Holy Spirit is living within these people. When they preach in the power of the Holy Spirit, those who believe will be forgiven. Those who hear the Word of God spoken in the power of the Spirit, have first-hand experience of God. If they reject the Word, their sins are not forgiven, because God has personally offered them forgiveness and they refused it. The disciples are God's representatives on earth, not just because He sends them, but because He goes with them. What they offer, He offers, and what they give, He gives.

> *24But Thomas, one of the twelve, called Didymus, was not with them when Jesus came. 25The other disciples therefore said unto him, We have seen the Lord. But he said unto them, Except I shall see in his hands the*

*print of the nails, and put my hand into his side, I will
not believe.*

26And after eight days

Was this the Jewish Monday, but our Sunday night?

*again his disciples were within, and Thomas with
them.*

What had the disciples been doing for eight days? Perhaps praying, adjusting, learning from the Spirit who now dwelled in them. Jesus was not physically present, but already His Spirit was in ten of the eleven.

*Jesus cometh, the doors being shut, and stood in the
midst, and said, Peace be unto you. 27Then saith he
to Thomas, Reach hither thy finger, and see my hands;
and reach hither thy hand, and put it into my side:
and be not faithless, but believing. 28Thomas answered and said unto him, My Lord and my God.
29Jesus saith unto him, Because thou hast seen me,
thou hast believed: blessed are they that have not
seen, and yet have believed.*

Thomas is the cautionary tale for those who refuse to believe because they did not personally witness Jesus after the resurrection. The Lord granted Thomas' demand. Thomas saw the risen Lord. Did the Lord make Thomas touch the wounds?

What happened to the Lord and the disciples in the eight days between Easter and the Lord's appearance to Thomas and the others? Was the Lord visiting others who needed to see Him – His brothers John and Jude perhaps? His mother? Much may have transpired on earth, not recorded in the gospels. Perhaps the gospel writers didn't even hear about all the other incidents. God is always working, even though only fragments of what He has done are recorded for us in the Bible. It is the same today. God is at work, even though the recording of His work in the Bible is closed. We are seeing it and experiencing it all play out before our eyes. We are witnesses to the truth of the Gospel.

What did Thomas do during those eight days? The other disciples were filled with joy. Did Thomas question his unbelief? For eight days Thomas was in the presence of the first people ever to be indwelt by the Holy Spirit. What did he think and experience? Surely one reason Jesus waited eight days was because Thomas needed eight days. ... "suddenly ... Jesus was standing among them." (NLT.) That's how close Heaven is – it's right there.

> *30Many other signs therefore did Jesus in the presence of the disciples, which are not written in this book: 31but these are written, that ye may believe that Jesus is the Christ, the Son of God; and that believing ye may have life in his name.*

Verses 30 and 31 address the whole life on earth of Jesus recorded in the gospel of John; so that we, unlike Thomas, will believe in Jesus based on the testimony of others, though we have not seen Him. "... so that [we] may continue to believe ..." over the generations since Jesus walked on earth and John told the story, "... and that by believing in Him [we] will have life by the power of His name." (NLT.) John's original audience might have been believers, but Jesus began immediately to use this gospel record to save people who had never heard before. How many people have come to faith while reading the Gospel of John? Jesus' power and the power of the Holy Spirit are released on people while they read this book.

Chapter 21: You, you follow Me.

John 21 (ASV) 1After these things Jesus manifested himself again to the disciples at the sea of Tiberias; and he manifested himself on this wise. 2There was together Simon Peter, and Thomas called Didymus, and Nathanael of Cana in Galilee, and the sons of Zebedee, and two other of his disciples. 3Simon Peter saith unto them, I go a fishing. They say unto him, We also come with thee. They went forth, and entered into the boat; and that night they took nothing. 4But when day was now breaking, Jesus stood on the beach: yet the disciples knew not that it was Jesus. 5Jesus therefore saith unto them, Children, have ye aught to eat? They answered him, No. 6And he said unto them, Cast the net on the right side of the boat, and ye shall find. They cast therefore, and now they were not able to draw it for the multitude of fishes. 7That disciple therefore whom Jesus loved saith unto Peter, It is the Lord. So when Simon Peter heard that it was the Lord, he girt his coat about him (for he was naked), and cast himself into the sea. 8But the other disciples came in the little boat (for they were not far from the land, but about two hundred cubits off), dragging the net full of fishes.

Peter had returned to Galilee and the life he knew before Jesus. He was awaiting Jesus' instructions, but the idea of settling back into his old life must have been tempting. In response, Jesus reenacted Peter's original call with another miraculous catch of fishes.

> *9So when they got out upon the land, they see a fire of coals there, and fish laid thereon, and bread. 10Jesus saith unto them, Bring of the fish which ye have now taken. 11Simon Peter therefore went up, and drew the net to land, full of great fishes, a hundred and fifty and three: and for all there were so many, the net was not rent.*

Jesus already had breakfast cooking when the disciples arrived with the fish, but Jesus used their fish, too. Jesus didn't need their efforts, but He used them anyway. And Jesus served them breakfast. What a Savior! This is how the Lord treats us. He adds our meagre efforts to His effectual ones, and then He celebrates His success as though it were ours. He who never grows weary takes care of us.

> *12Jesus saith unto them, Come and break your fast. And none of the disciples durst inquire of him, Who art thou? knowing that it was the Lord. 13Jesus cometh, and taketh the bread, and giveth them, and the fish likewise.*

Why does John bother to mention that no one dared to ask Him who He was? Not because it is necessary to the story, but because it was part of the experience, part of what they all felt at the time. And remember, they had been up all night fishing. They weren't feeling all that chipper. That's why Jesus was taking care of breakfast.

> *14This is now the third time that Jesus was manifested to the disciples, after that he was risen from the dead.*

This was the "third time" Jesus had appeared to these disciples since the resurrection. Probably not much time had elapsed since the resurrection. In Matthew 28:7 the angel says Jesus is going ahead of them into Galilee and they will see Him there. An interesting connection, since it doesn't appear in John 21 that Matthew was in the boat. Could the other two in the boat have been Andrew and Phillip? All eleven might have gone to Galilee, but not all of them were fishermen. As Acts 1:1-9 records, Jesus saw them all on other occasions.

Combining the gospel narratives, it seems Jesus appeared to His followers during that eight days or so while the disciples were in Jerusalem; then He sent them to Galilee and taught them there; then He sent them back to Jerusalem, and taught them there, before He ascended, at the end of 40 days. Matthew 28, the "Great Commission" is given in Galilee. Luke 24 and Acts 1 show the ascension to have been near Jerusalem. Why did Jesus have them coming and going while He prepared them to take over His ministry? One, it was how He had taught them during the previous three years. Two, it gave them something to do with their bodies while He filled their minds and hearts. Three, it protected them from the authorities' notice. Had they stayed in one place they would have aroused notice and perhaps arrest.

> *15So when they had broken their fast, Jesus saith to Simon Peter, Simon, son of John, lovest thou me more than these? He saith unto him, Yea, Lord; thou knowest that I love thee. He saith unto him, Feed my lambs. 16He saith to him again a second time, Simon, son of John, lovest thou me? He saith unto him, Yea, Lord;*

thou knowest that I love thee. He saith unto him, Tend my sheep. 17He saith unto him the third time, Lovest thou me? And he said unto him, Lord, thou knowest all things; thou knowest that I love thee. Jesus saith unto him, Feed my sheep.

How deeply Peter must have felt his failure of the past and his inadequacy for the future. But Jesus trusted him with His church.

18Verily, verily, I say unto thee, When thou wast young, thou girdedst thyself, and walkedst whither thou wouldest: but when thou shalt be old, thou shalt stretch forth thy hands, and another shall gird thee, and carry thee whither thou wouldest not. 19Now this he spake, signifying by what manner of death he should glorify God. And when he had spoken this, he saith unto him, Follow me.

The way Jesus focuses on Peter is interesting, both to restore him and to commission him. I guess Peter never faltered in his faith after this breakfast with Jesus. Peter's identity had always been as a Galilean and a fisherman. Now he would be the Lord's and go wherever the Lord sent him. He would say, do, and be things a Galilean fisherman would not.

20Peter, turning about, seeth the disciple whom Jesus loved following; who also leaned back on his breast at the supper, and said, Lord, who is he that betrayeth thee? 21Peter therefore seeing him saith to Jesus, Lord, and what shall this man do? 22Jesus saith unto him, If I will that he tarry till I come, what is that to thee? Follow thou me. 23This saying therefore went forth among the brethren, that that disciple should not die: yet Jesus said not unto him, that he should not die; but, If I will that he tarry till I come, what is that to thee?

24This is the disciple that beareth witness of these things, and wrote these things: and we know that his witness is true.

What about John? Jesus had a different, but equally definite plan for his future. And the church that witnessed John's writing his gospel testified in support of him and the authority of his book. The people of this church knew John and the evidence they offer has weight.

25And there are also many other things which Jesus did, the which if they should be written every one, I suppose that even the world itself would not contain the books that should be written.

In reflecting on Jesus and His significance to history, John could not resist the final accolade – all the books in the world cannot describe the importance of this Man's life. Jesus did "many other things," and He is doing them still!

Warnock Pro and Bernard MT Condensed on LSI archival créme white
Type and Design by Karen Paul Stone